John Murray

Agamemnon of Aeschylus and the Bacchanals of Euripides

With Passages from the Lyric and Later Poets of Greece

John Murray

Agamemnon of Aeschylus and the Bacchanals of Euripides
With Passages from the Lyric and Later Poets of Greece

ISBN/EAN: 9783744768757

Printed in Europe, USA, Canada, Australia, Japan

Cover: Foto ©ninafisch / pixelio.de

More available books at **www.hansebooks.com**

THE
AGAMEMNON OF ÆSCHYLUS
AND THE BACCHANALS
OF EURIPIDES

WITH

*PASSAGES FROM THE LYRIC AND
LATER POETS OF GREECE*

TRANSLATED BY

HENRY HART MILMAN, D.D.

DEAN OF ST. PAUL'S

LONDON
JOHN MURRAY, ALBEMARLE STREET
1865

PREFACE.

WITH the exception of the Tragedies (only passages of which I had rendered), almost all the Translations in this volume were interspersed in the Lectures which I delivered as Professor of Poetry in Oxford. My object was to enliven Lectures then composed, according to ancient and rigid usage, in Latin: for the perfect familiarity with Latin, which would enable the audience to follow an unbroken Lecture in that language, was by no means general, especially among the younger students.

The subject of my Lectures was the History of Greek Poetry. Since that time (between thirty and forty years ago) the Histories of Greek Poetry by Bode, Ulrici, above all the great work of Otfried Müller (translated by the late lamented Sir G. Cornewall Lewis), and the History of Greek Literature by our accomplished countryman, my friend Colonel Mure, had not appeared. Conscious of the deficiencies of my own Sketch, I have consigned my Lectures with unaverted eyes to the flames.

The Translations, however, I was not quite so easily content to part with. They were heard at the time with much favour by many whose judgment stood high in the University, and I have met with some in later days (one especially by whose brilliant and busy life such reminiscences, I should have supposed, would have been long and utterly effaced) who retained a vivid impression of the delight with which they had heard them in their youth. To these (few I fear) as to myself they may be welcome, as pleasant voices from days long gone by; while to some others (not, I fear, too many), lovers of Greek Poetry especially, they may be not altogether unacceptable.

· DEANERY, ST. PAUL'S,
Christmas 1865.

The Engravings are all from the Antique.

CONTENTS.

	Page
THE AGAMEMNON	1
THE BACCHANALS	95
FRAGMENTS FROM THE LYRIC POETS	185
Bacchylides	191
Simonides	193
FRAGMENTS FROM THE ELEGIAC POETS—	
Theognis	195
Solon	197
FRAGMENTS FROM THE TRAGEDIANS—	
Æschylus	198
Sophocles	209
Euripides	212
FRAGMENTS FROM THE COMEDY—	
Aristophanes	220
FRAGMENTS FROM THE LATER COMEDY	225
FRAGMENTS FROM THE LYRIC POETS	226

CONTENTS.

	Page
FRAGMENTS FROM THE PHILOSOPHIC POETS	237

FRAGMENTS FROM THE LATER POETS—

Onomacritus	245
Apollonius Rhodius	248
Callimachus	254
Lycophron	257
Theocritus	258
Moschus	260
Aratus	261
Dionysius	263
Oppian	265
Nicander	270

ANTHOLOGIA—

Meleager	273
Rufinus	274
Agathias	274
Meleager	275
Nicias	276
Æsopus	277
Palladas	277

LOCAL INSCRIPTIONS	278

VOTIVE INSCRIPTIONS—

Simonides	280
Mnasalcas	280
Anyta	281
Macedonius	281

	Page
VOTIVE INSCRIPTIONS—	
Antipater . .	282
Phanius	283
Agathias	283
DEDICATORY—	
Bacchylides	284
INSCRIPTIONS RELATING TO THE FINE ARTS . .	286
EPITAPHIA . .	292
HYMNS . . .	295
QUINTUS CALABER . . .	298
TRYPHIODORUS	306
COLUTHUS . . .	308
MUSÆUS . . .	310
NONNUS	312

THE AGAMEMNON.

THE AGAMEMNON.

Very many years ago I had translated parts of the *Agamemnon*. I have been tempted by the surpassing grandeur of the Drama, the *Macbeth* of antiquity, to complete the work. In the passages formerly rendered, I had generally followed the readings and interpretations of the editions in the highest estimation at that time, those of Porson (the text), Schütz, and Blomfield. I have now consulted some of the later editions, especially the copious notes of Dr. Peile, in which are embodied much of Wellauer, Klausen, O. Müller, and Dindorf. I have, in the many passages which are still left in great part to conjecture, adopted that sense or reading which appeared to me the best and most poetical. Possibly I may have chosen some, as most poetical and Æschylean, which the severer scholar may question or reject. The peculiar manner and wonderful power of Æschylus in suggesting, rather than developing or distinctly expressing, many thoughts and many images by a few pregnant and close-set words, or by an overteeming compound epithet, sometimes compel the translator, if he would not lose the full force of the poetry, to indulge in paraphrase beyond what his judgment would allow in other cases. I have abstained from looking into other translations except that of Mr. Symmons of Christ Church (1824), the Notes of which show scholarship of a very high order, and a very fine and just appreciation of the poetry of Æschylus. If Mr. Symmons had not indulged in paraphrase to an extent, at least to me, not justifiable even in the rendering of Æschylus, and had been gifted with a finer ear for lyric harmony, his version would have been excellent.

DRAMATIS PERSONÆ.

The Watchman.
Chorus of aged Argives.
Clytemnestra.
Talthybius, *the Herald.*
Agamemnon.
Cassandra.
Ægisthus.

THE AGAMEMNON.

THE WATCHMAN.

GRANT, O ye Gods! a respite from this toil:
Night after night, this livelong year, I've sate
Couched like a watch-dog on the palace roof
Of Atreus' son, and viewed yon starry conclave,
Those glorious dynasts of the sky, that bear
Winter and summer round to mortal men.
And still the signal lamp I watch, the fire
That shall flame forth intelligence from Troy—
The tidings of her capture. So commands
Our Queen's unfeminine soul, with hope elate.
  And while my night-perturbed and dew-dank couch
I keep, by gentle dreams unvisited,
Fear still usurps the place of sleep, nor leaves
My weary eyes to close in lasting slumber.

Still, as I strive to guile the unquiet night—
Sad remedy!—with song or carol gay,
I can but weep and mourn this fatal house,
Not as of old with righteous wisdom ruled.
   Come thou, my toils release! break forth, break
      forth
From darkness, fiery messenger of joy!
   All hail, thou glory of the night! that blazest
With noon-day splendour, wakening Argos up
To dance and song for this thrice-blest event!

         What, ho! what, ho!
Loud do I cry to Agamemnon's queen,
Swift leaping from her bed, to shriek aloud
Through all the palace her exultant hymn
To this auspicious lamp, since Troy's proud walls
Have fallen! So tells yon blazing beacon-fire.
   I the glad prelude will begin, and hail
This best good fortune of our lord : the dice
Could cast no luckier throw than yon bright beacon.
   O that this hand may grasp the gracious hand
Of Argos' king, returning to his home!
But peace! no more! the seal is on my lips!
The palace self, could it but find a voice,
Would speak from its dark walls! To the under-
      standing
I speak; to those who understand not—nothing.

CHORUS.

Lo the tenth year since Priam's 'vengeful foes,
King Agamemnon and King Menelaus, rose,
Since that twin-throned, twin-sceptred pair,
Like two strong coursers in one battle-car,
Saw in close ranks their kindred squadrons meet;
And proud set forth the thousand-galleyed fleet;
And loud and fierce their battle-clang,
Like screams of angry vultures rang:
They for their plunder'd brood distrest
Wheel round and round the rifled nest;
And high on oary wings up-borne,
Their wasted toil o'er their lost fledgelings mourn.

But some avenging God above—
Apollo, Pan, or mightiest Jove—
Hearing the shrilly-piercing cry
Of those plumed wanderers of the sky,
Sends down the avenging Fury dread
To blast the spoiler's guilty head.
Thus highest Hospitable Jove
Did the twin sons of Atreus move
Against the adulterous Phrygian boy,
Dooming alike to Greece and Troy
For that too-often wedded wife
Many a wild and wearying strife,
With failing knees bowed to the dust,
And lances shivering in their onward thrust.

But be the issue as it may,
Eternal Fate will hold its way;
Nor lips that pray, nor eyes that weep,
Nor cups that rich libations steep,
Soothe those dark Powers' relentless ire,
Whose altars never flame with hallowed fire.

But we, unhonour'd in our age,
Unfit the glorious war to wage,
Propp'd on our staves, remain alone,
And drag our second childhood on.
The strength in infant limbs which reigns,
And that which chills our aged veins,
Awakes not at the battle-cry;
For age, whose leaf is sere and dry,
Thin as a vision seen by day,
Crawls on three feet on its decrepit way.

Daughter of Tyndarus! but thou,
O Clytemnestra, answer now!
Are glad and glorious tidings thine?
That hurrying thus from shrine to shrine;
To all the Gods that guard our land
Thou bid'st the votive victim stand,
And fires upon the altar glow
To Gods above and Gods below;
And here and there to heaven flame up
The blazing lamps, whose mantling cup

With blameless oil is running o'er,
Brought from the inmost royal store.
  Tell, O queen, what may be told;
What our ears may hear, unfold,
And calm our agonising care,
That struggles still with drear despair;
And now consoled by that soft light
From every altar beaming bright,
Sees Hope appear, and smile relief
Upon our soul-consuming grief.

Power is upon me now, to sing the awful sign
  That cross'd the warrior monarchs on their road;
Heaven breathes within the 'suasive song divine,
  And strength through my rapt soul is pour'd abroad.
    The birds I sing, whose fateful flight
    Sent forth the twin-throned Argive might,
And all the youth of Greece, a gallant crew,
    With spear in each avenging hand,
    Against the guilty Trojan land.
Even at the threshold of the palace, flew
    The king of birds o'er either king,
    One black and one with snow-white wing,
Rightward, on the hand that grasps the spear,
Down through the glittering courts they steer,
    Swooping the hare's prolific brood,
    No more to crop its grassy food.
Ring out the dolorous hymn, yet triumph still the good!

But the wise seer, in his prophetic view,
　　When he the twin-soul'd sons of Atreus saw,
At once the feasters on the hares he knew,
　　Those leaders of the host, then broke his words of
　　　　awe :—
" In time old Priam's city wall
　　Before that conquering host shall fall,
　　And all within her towers lie waste ;
　　Her teeming wealth of man and beast
　　Shall Fate in her dire violence destroy ;
　　May ne'er heaven's envy, like a cloud,
　　So darken o'er that army proud,
　　　　The fine-forged curb of Troy !
　　For Artemis, with jealous ire,
　　Beholds the winged hounds of her great sire
　　Swooping the innocent leverets' scarce-born brood,
　　And loathes the eagles' feast of blood.
Ring out the dolorous hymn, yet triumph still the good !

" Such is that beauteous Goddess' love
　　To the strong lion's callow brood,
　　And all that, the green meadows wont to rove,
　　　　From the full udder quaff the liquid food.
　　O Goddess ! though thy wrath reprove
Those savage birds, yet turn those awful signs to good !

" But, Io Pæan ! now I cry ;
　　May ne'er her injured deity,

With adverse fleet-emprisoning blast
The unpropitious sky o'ercast;
   Hastening that other sacrifice—
That darker sacrifice, unblest
By music or by jocund feast:
   Whence sad domestic strife shall rise,
And, dreadless of her lord, fierce woman's hate;
Whose child-avenging wrath in sullen state
Broods, wily housewife, in her chamber's gloom,
   Over that unforgotten doom."

Such were the words that Calchas clanged abroad,
When crossed those ominous birds the onward road
   Of that twice royal brotherhood:
     A mingled doom
   Of glory and of gloom.
Ring out the dolorous hymn, yet triumph still the good!

   Whoe'er thou art, great Power above,
   If that dread name thou best approve,
   All duly weighed I cannot find,
   Unburthening my o'er-loaded mind,
A mightier name than that of mightiest Jove.
     He, that so great of old,
   Branched out in strength invincible and bold,
     Is nothing now. Who after came
     Before the victor sank to shame:
Most wise is he who sings the all-conquering might of Jove.

Jove, that great God
Who taught to mortals wisdom's road;
By whose eternal rule
Adversity is grave instruction's school.
In the calm hour of sleep
Conscience, the sad remembrancer, will creep
To the inmost heart, and there enforce
On the reluctant spirit the wisdom of remorse.
Mighty the grace of those dread deities,
Throned on their judgment bench, high in the empyrean
skies!

Nor then did the elder chief, in sooth,
Of all the Achean youth,
Dare brand with blame the holy seer;
When adverse fortune 'gan to veer,
Emprisoning that becalmed host
On Chalcis' coast,
Where the heavy refluent billows roar
'Gainst Aulis' rock-bound shore.

And long and long from wintry Strymon blew
The weary, hungry, anchor-straining blasts,
The winds that wandering seamen dearly rue,
Nor spared the cables worn and groaning masts;
And, lingering on in indolent delay,
Slow wasted all the strength of Greece away.

But when the shrill-voiced prophet 'gan proclaim
   That remedy more dismal and more dread,
     Than the drear weather blackening overhead ;
And spoke in Artemis' most awful name,
The sons of Atreus, 'mid their armed peers,
Their sceptres dashed to earth, and each broke out in
        tears,
   And thus the elder king began to say :
    "Dire doom! to disobey the Gods' commands!
More dire, my child, mine house's pride, to slay,
   Dabbling in virgin blood a father's hands.
   Alas! alas! which way to fly?
   As base deserter quit the host,
   The pride and strength of our great league all lost?
Should I the storm-appeasing rite deny,
Will not their wrathfullest wrath rage up and swell—
Exact the virgin's blood?—oh, would 'twere o'er and
        well!"

So 'neath Necessity's stern yoke he passed,
   And his lost soul, with impious impulse veering,
Surrendered to the accurst unholy blast,
   Warped to the dire extreme of human daring.
     The frenzy of affliction still
      Maddens, dire counsellor, man's soul to ill.

So he endured to be the priest
In that child-slaughtering rite unblest,

The first-fruit offering of that host
In fatal war for a bad woman lost.
The prayers, the mute appeal to her hard sire,
　　Her youth, her virgin beauty,
Nought heeded they, the Chiefs for war on fire.
　　So to the ministers of that dire duty
　　(First having prayed) the father gave the sign,
Like some soft kid, to lift her to the shrine.

　　　There lay she prone,
　Her graceful garments round her thrown;
　　But first her beauteous mouth around
　　　Their violent bonds they wound,
Lest her dread curse the fated house should smite
　　With their rude inarticulate might.
But she her saffron robe to earth let fall:
　　The shaft of pity from her eye
Transpierced that awful priesthood—one and all.
　　Lovely as in a picture stood she by
As she would speak. Thus at her father's feasts
The virgin, 'mid the revelling guests,
Was wont with her chaste voice to supplicate
For her dear father an auspicious fate.

I saw no more! to speak more is not mine;
Not unfulfilled was Chalcas lore divine.
　　　Eternal justice still will bring
　　　　Wisdom out of suffering.

So to the fond desire farewell,
The inevitable future to foretell;
    'Tis but our woe to antedate;
Joint knit with joint, expands the full-formed fate.
    Yet at the end of these dark days
May prospering weal return at length;
    Thus in his spirit prays
He of the Apian land the sole remaining strength.

CLYTEMNESTRA *enters.*

CHORUS.

I come, O Clytemnestra, to salute
Thy majesty! 'Tis meet the wife to honour
When vacant of its lord the kingly throne.
Fain would I know, what thou hast heard, what
    heard not.
Greet'st thou with incense some glad messenger?
Yet dare I not, if silent, blame thy silence.

CLYTEMNESTRA.

With joyful tidings, as the proverb says,
Dawns forth the Morning from her mother Night.
Thou shalt hear things passing thine utmost hope:
The Argive host hath taken Priam's city.

CHORUS.

What say'st thou? I can scarce believe thy words.

CLYTEMNESTRA.

The Greeks are lords of Troy! Speak I not clear

CHORUS.

So great my joy, I cannot choose but weep!

CLYTEMNESTRA.

Thy tears bear witness to thy loyalty.

CHORUS.

Is the proof credible of this great fact?

CLYTEMNESTRA.

It is. Why not? Doth the God e'er deceive?

CHORUS.

Art thou beguiled by phantom shapes of dreams?

CLYTEMNESTRA.

I care not for the mind that's drenched in sleep.

CHORUS.

Hath made thee wanton some swift sudden voice?

CLYTEMNESTRA.

Mock'st me, as thou would mock a simple girl?

CHORUS.

How long is't since the ruined city fell?

CLYTEMNESTRA.

This day, I say, born of this very night.

CHORUS.

What messenger hath hither flown so swiftly?

CLYTEMNESTRA.

The Fire-God, kindling his bright light on Ida!
Beacon to beacon fast and forward flashed,
An estafette of fire, on to the rocks
Of Hermes-hallowed Lemnos: from that isle
Caught, thirdly, Jove-crowned Athos the red light,
That broader, skimming o'er the shimmering sea,
Went travelling in its strength. For our delight
The pine-torch, golden-glittering like the sun,
Spoke to the watchman on Macistus' height.
Nor he delaying, nor by careless sleep
Subdued, sent on the fiery messenger:
Far o'er Euripus' tide the beacon-blaze
Signalled to the Messapian sentinels.
Light answering light, they sent the tidings on,
Kindling into a blaze the old dry heath;
And mightier still, and waning not a whit,
The light leaped o'er Asopus' plain, most like
The crescent moon, on to Cithæron's peak,
And woke again another missive fire.
Nor did the guard disdain the far-seen light,

But kindled up at once a mightier flame.
O'er the Gorgopian lake it flashed like lightning
On the sea-beaten cliffs of Megaris;
Woke up the watchman not to spare his fire,
And, gathering in its unexhausted strength,
The long-waving bearded flame from off the cliffs
That overlook the deep Saronian gulf,
As from a mirror streamed. On flashed it; reached
Arachne, our close neighbouring height, and there,
Not unbegotten of that bright fire on Ida,
On sprang it to Atrides' palace roof.
Such were the laws of those swift beacon-fires:
So flash the torches on from hand to hand
In the holy rite, brightest the first and last.
Such is the proof and sign of victory
Sent by my husband from now captured Troy.

CHORUS.

O woman, to the Gods ere long I'll pray.
But lost in wonder at thy words of joy,
Fain would I hear them, at full length, again.

CLYTEMNESTRA.

This day the Argives are the lords of Troy;
A wild and dissonant cry rises, I ween,
From all the city. Vinegar and oil,
Poured in one vessel, mingle not, but stand
In discord obstinate: so may be heard

The voices of the conquerors and the vanquished
In awful opposition.   Prostrate these
Over the reeking bodies of the slain,
Husbands or brothers ; children, cowering low
O'er their dead parents, now no more to lift
Their heads in freedom, wail their best beloved.
Those weary with the night-wandering toil of war,
Break their long fast with what the city yields,
Not orderly apportioned, but as each
Has drawn his lot, at feast upon the spoil.
And in the palaces of captive Troy
They take their ease ; under the frosty heaven
No more, nor shivering with the cold dank dews,
Unguarded sleep they through the happy night.
If reverently ye adore Troy's tutelar gods—
Gods of the vanquished land, and the holy shrines—
Captors, ye 'll not be captives in your turn.
Oh, may no lawless lust our host invade,
Ravening for spoil, slaves of base thirst for gain !
Yet have they, ere their safe return to home,
One half of their long stadium's course to run,
And even if guiltless come the army back ;
Be there no new offence ; Troy's carnage still
May reek to heaven and wake the avenging Gods.
These are a woman's words, may good prevail,
And the swung balance in our favour turn.
'Tis this of all heaven's blessings I would choose.

CHORUS.

Woman, like a wise man thou speakest wisely.
With these unanswerable proofs content,
I gird me for thanksgiving to the Gods;—
A glorious guerdon this of all our toils.

CHORUS.

O monarch Jove! O friendly Night,
Rich in ten thousand treasures bright!
That over Troy's proud towers hast cast
The net of ruin strong and vast;
None—none, may 'scape—nor young nor great—
The meshes of all-sweeping Fate.
Before great Jove I bow the knee,
The god of hospitality.
'Gainst guilty Paris long ago,
Uplift he held the home-drawn bow—
The bolt of fate
Nor lingered late,
Nor meteor-like was lost on high,
Over the stars up in the sightless sky.

STROPHE.

They have it—Jove's red shaft of wrath—
I track it on its fiery path:
He decreed and it was done.
Heaven marks that race from son to son

(Who says the Gods of the impious take no care,
Treading forbidden ground) fierce wars who dare
    Breathe in insufferable haughtiness,
    And in o'er-boiling insolent excess,
Glorious beyond all good. Be mine the better part,
    Such as contents the wise of heart.
Still moderate unendangered health.
    To him there is no tower of wealth
Who with his scornful heel strikes down the shrine
    Of justice all divine.

ANTISTROPHE.

But that stern counsellor of fate,
Persuasion, keeps her violent state.

There is no remedy of worth.
It is not veiled—the light breaks forth—
That baleful star, with its disastrous rays,
As the base brass by touchstone tried betrays
    The black within—since that perfidious boy,
    Hunting the bird down in his wanton joy,
Did miserable doom to his lost city bear.
    (There was no God to hear the prayer.)
The unjust, the author of all woe,
    Ever brings ruin. Paris so
Defiled Atrides' hospitable house
    Stealing the adulterous spouse.

STROPHE.

Bequeathing the wild fray to her own nation
  Of clashing spears, and the embattled fleet,
Bearing to Troy her dowry—desolation,
  She glided through the gate with noiseless feet,
Daring the undareable! But in their grief
  Deep groaned the prophets of that ancient race:
"Woe to the palace! woe to its proud Chief,
  The bed warm with the husband's fond embrace!"
    Silent there she stood,
Too false to honour, too fair to revile;
  For her, far off over the ocean flood,
Yet still most lovely in her parting smile,
  A spectre queens it in that haunted spot.

Odious, in living beauty's place,
Is the cold statue's fine-wrought grace.
Where speaking eyes are wanting, love is not.

ANTISTROPHE.

And phantasms, from his deep distress unfolding,
　Are ever present with their idle charms.
And when that beauteous form he seems beholding,
　It slides away from out his clasping arms.
The vision! in an instant it is gone,
　On light wing down the silent paths of sleep!
Around that widowed heart, so mute, so lone.
　Such are the griefs, and griefs than these more deep
　　　To all from Greece that part
For the dread warfare: Patient in her gloom,
　Sits Sorrow, guardian god of each sad home,
And many woes pierce rankling every heart.
Oh, well each knew the strong, the brave, the just,
　Whom they sent forth on the horrid track
　Of battle; and what now comes back?
Their vacant armour, and a little dust!

STROPHE.

But Mars, who barters human lives for gold,
　And holds the scales in the wild war of spears,
Sends home from Ilion a thin remnant cold,
　Saved from the pyre, too slight to waken tears:

And for the warriors bold returns
A few dull ashes in their fine-wrought urns.
   Here in sad eloquence they tell
Of him most skilful in the battle's strife—
   Of him who in his glory fell,
Slain for another's guilty wife.
      In silent murmurs low
      Thus speaks the general woe
Against the kings of Atreus' race,
In the fierce battlefield who took their place,
    Leaders of the avenging host.
    Some all along far Ilion's coast,
Cut off in their young beauty's bloom,
Under Troy's walls found their untimely tomb,
Whom a strange hostile soil and hurried rites inhume.

ANTISTROPHE.

The heavy burthen of a people's curse
   Runs through the city, the dread debt to pay
Of hoarded hate. In my soul's depths I nurse
   A brooding fear, midnight will not betray.
The almighty Gods are never blind
To the wide-wasting slaughterers of their kind.
   The black Erynnyes, with Time,
Their awful colleague, on the topmost height
   Of their full pride, the men of crime,
Drive backward to the abyss, where might

Is none; down, deeper down,
  Where all things are unknown.
To those whose fame resounds too loud
Jove's bolt bursts blinding from the thunder-cloud.
  Mine be the unenvied fate,
  Not too wealthy, not too great.
I covet not, not I, the bad renown
To be the sacker of another's town,
Or see, a wretched slave, the sacking of mine own.

CHORUS.

Through all the city the glad rumour flies
Of th' herald lights that flash along the skies.
If true, who knows? from heaven? or but a lie?
  Who such a child, so 'reft of sense,
  To kindle at the glad intelligence;
And when the change comes o'er the tidings fair,
To die away in dull despair.
'Tis woman's nature foremost to descry
  Ere it arrives, the ill, with instinct sure
  The joy unripe and premature.
By woman only vouched, the tale of glory
Dies out at once, a soon-forgotten story.

CLYTEMNESTRA.

Soon shall we know of those bright flashing lights,
These intercommuning red beacon-fires,
If they be true, or like delusive dreams

Have these joy-breathing lights the soul beguiled.
I see upon yon shore a herald shaded
With olive-branches; and a second witness,
The thirsty dust, brother of mire, I see,
Not voiceless, though he speaks not in the language
Of fire-smoke on the forest mountain-tops,
He with his words will ratify our joy.
I loathe the thought that he will dash our hopes,
And yet our dubious joy may bear increase.
     [CLYTEMNESTRA *retires.*

CHORUS.

May he that otherwise prays for our city
Reap the sad harvest of a broken heart!

The HERALD *enters.*

HERALD.

Ho, native Argos! my paternal soil!
Ho, my dear country! The tenth year hath dawned
Since I forsook thee. After the dire wreck
Of many hopes, this is at length fulfilled.
I dared not dream that in this Argive land
I should repose in a dear quiet grave.
 Hail, land beloved! all hail, thou glorious sun!
Jove, our land's sovereign! and thou, Pythian king!
On us no more shall shower your baleful shafts.
Long, long enough upon Scamander's banks

Did'st thou come, darkling in thine ire! Be now
Our saviour, Lord of our high festivals!
O king Apollo! All the gods I call
That o'er our games preside; and chiefly thee,
Our tutelar, the herald Hermes! him
Whom heralds worship with devoutest love;
And ye who sent us forth, the heroes old,
Receive our host, all the foe's lance has spared.

  Ho, palace of our kings! Ho, roofs beloved!
The venerable seats of justice! Gods
Whose images stand glittering in the sun!
Now, now, if ever, with bright-beaming eyes
Welcome our king, after long years returned.
He comes, King Agamemnon, like the dawn
Out of the darkness; for to us, to all
That host around, he brings the common joy.

  Greet, greet him nobly. Is't not well to greet
Him who the firm foundations of old Troy
Dug up with the avenging spade of Jove,
Searching the soil down to its deepest roots?
The altars and the temples of their gods
Are all in shapeless ruin; all the seed
Utterly withered from the blasted land.
Such is the yoke, that o'er the towers of Troy
Hath thrown that elder chieftain, Atreus' son.

  Blest above mortals, lo, he comes! Of men
Now living, who so worthy of all honour?
Paris no more, and his accomplice city

Shall vaunt their proud pathetic tragedy:
Of robbery and of foul ravishment
Found guilty. With all-wasting Ruin's scythe
Hath he mowed down his father's ancient house.
Priam and his sons have double forfeit paid.

CHORUS.

Hail, and rejoice, herald of the Argive host!

HERALD.

Rejoice! Were it God's will, I'd die on the instant.

CHORUS.

Love of thy native land hath tried thee sore.

HERALD.

So that I cannot choose but weep for joy.

CHORUS.

Wert thou then wounded by that sweet disease?

HERALD.

What mean'st? Teach me to master this thy speech.

CHORUS.

Smitten with love of those who loved no less.

HERALD.

Say'st thou the city mourned us in our absence?

CHORUS.

With many sighs from our heart's secret **depths.**

HERALD.

Why secret was this **sorrow for our host?**

CHORUS.

Peace!   Silence **is the best of remedies.**

HERALD.

Whom, when our kings were absent, did ye dread?

CHORUS.

Even as ye now may dread : death had been mercy.

HERALD.

'Tis well! all well! in the long range of time.
One man may say, things turn out right, **while others**
Heap them with blame.   Who, but the Gods in heaven,
Lives through all ages without sin or **woe?**
  If I should tell our toils and weary watchings,
Rare landings, sleep snatched on the hard planks. What
   hour
Had not its dreary lot of wretchedness?

On land worse sufferings than the worst at sea.
Our beds were strewn under the hostile walls;
And from the skies, and from the fenny land,
Came dripping the chill dews, rotting our clothes,
Matting our hair, like hides of shaggy beasts.
Our winters shall I tell, when the bleak cold
Intolerable, down from Ida's snows
Came rushing; even the birds fell dead around us.
Or summer heats, when on his mid-day couch
Heavily fell the waveless sea, no breath
Stirring the sultry air. Why grieve we now?
All is gone by! the toils all o'er! the dead!
No thought have they of rising from their graves.
Why count the suffrages of those who have fallen?
The living only, fickle fortune's wrath
Afflicts with grief. I to calamity
Have bid a long farewell. Of the Argive host
To us, the few survivors, our rich gains
Weigh down in the scale our poor uncounted losses.
In the face of the noon-day sun we make our boast,
Flying abroad over the sea and land,
That now the Argive host hath taken Troy;
And in the ancestral temples of their Gods
Have nailed the spoils for our eternal glory.

CHORUS.

I doubt no longer, by thy words subdued.
Old age is ever young to learn what's right.

THE AGAMEMNON.

But these things most concern Queen Clytemnestra,
Let her enjoy their glorious wealth with us.

CLYTEMNESTRA *enters.*

CLYTEMNESTRA.

Already have I shrieked in my wild joy,
When first the midnight fiery messenger
Came telling of the fall and sack of Troy.
Some girding said, " Thou by those beacon-fires
Deceived, believest in the ruin of Troy.
'Tis ever thus with woman, heart elate."
Deluded was I called in words like these;
Yet did I order instant sacrifice:
A woman gave the word; through all the city
The ululation ran with holy din,
Lulling the incense-fragrant fires that fed
On the hecatombs in the temples of the Gods.
Of this enough! from you I hear no more;
My lord the king himself shall tell the rest.
And I will haste, mine all-revered husband,
On his return, to meet with honour due.
To a wife's eye, what day so bright, so blessed,
As this which sees her meet her noble lord,
Under the Gods' protection home returned.
Throw wide the gates of welcome, tell my lord
Swiftly to come, and gladden the whole city;
So in his house he'll find his faithful wife,

Even as he left her, watchdog of the palace ;
Towards her lord of goodness unimpeached ;
Unloved of those alone who loved not him.
Ever the same, who **broke no single** seal
Of all his treasures in this length of **time.**
No pleasure have I known, but **thought of him ;**
Unsullied by ill fame, as the pure **brass**
Will take no stain or colouring from **the dye.**

HERALD.

A noble boast ! truth breathes in every word ;
How well doth it become a high-born woman !

CHORUS.

For mine instruction hath **she spoken thus,**
Clear words and plain, her soul's **interpreters.**
But tell me, Herald ! **of king Menelaus**
Fain would I hear. **Will he** return **in safety :**
He the delight and **bulwark of the land ?**

HERALD.

With pleasing falsehood **I** will not beguile you ;
Brief is the joy ye reap from such deceit.

CHORUS.

Good news and true ye speak not both at once ;
Ye cannot hide the mournful contradiction.

HERALD.

From the Greek host one man has disappeared,
He and his ship : I speak no falsehood now.

CHORUS.

Saw ye him first embark from Ilion ?
Or did one tempest scatter all the fleet ?

HERALD.

Like a skill'd archer thou hast hit the mark,
And in few words summ'd up a world of sorrow.

CHORUS.

What was the rumour that ran through the fleet ?
That he was living, or that he had perished ?

HERALD.

There's none can know, save the all-seeing Sun,
Whose light impregnates the whole teeming earth.

CHORUS.

By the Gods' wrath, a tempest smote the fleet ;
Say how it rose, and how it sank to peace.

HERALD.

'Twere ill to sully an auspicious day
With words of evil omen.   Different Gods

Have each their special honours. When there comes
A messenger with hateful countenance
Telling the abhorred fall of some great army,
A grievous wound to the whole commonwealth,
And many sons of many noble houses,
Victims piacular of cruel death,
Slain by that double scourge, dear to fierce Mars,
The twin-spear'd Fate, the bloody battle-team.
Sore over-laden by such woes as these,
'Tis meet we chant the Furies' doleful hymn.
I, the blest messenger of safety, come
To a glad city at high festival.
Mingling ill news with good. How shall I tell
The storm, not uncommissioned of Gods' wrath,
That wreck'd the Achæan fleet ; when those sworn foes,
Water and Fire, conspired and pledged their troth
Together to destroy the Argive host.
At night the billows in their fury rose,
Fierce blasts from Thrace against each other dash'd
The barks. They, butted as by battering-rams
By typhon whirlwinds and by rattling hail,
By that misguiding Shepherd driven amain,
Wander'd and disappear'd. But when the sun
Rose glorious in his full majestic light
We saw the Ægean, like a flowery mead,
With Argive corpses strew'd and drifting wrecks.
 But for our ship, our brave unshatter'd bark,
Some God (for surely 'twas no mortal power),

By stealth or by entreaty, from the jaws
Of ruin rescued, governing the helm :
And saviour Fortune sat upon the deck,
Doing the seamen's office. To the haven,
Where boil'd the sea no more, we glided in,
Nor stranded on the breaker-foaming shore.
How light and beautiful the day, when 'scaped
The hell of that vex'd sea, mistrusting still
Rude fortune, brooding o'er our bitter thoughts,
Vainly we sought to guile our grief, the host
All dead, and weltering in their billowy grave.
   And now, of these if one be breathing still,
They speak of us as lost. Why not? For we,
By a like fate think that they all have perished.
But all be for the best! Foremost and first
Look we for Menelaus' safe return.
If any sun-ray bright hath search'd him out,
Living and gazing on the light of day,
It is the provident care of Jove on high,
That will not utterly that royal race
Consume. So cherish we the lingering hope,
He may return to his ancestral house.
Thou hast heard all ; and all thou hast heard is true.

CHORUS.

STROPHE.

   Who the wondrous prophet, who
   With sagacious instinct true

(Was it the Unseen of mortal eye,
Who reads the book of destiny?)
Not by chance, but wisely weening
That dread name's mysterious meaning,
Her Helen call'd, the fated to destroy,
    Ships and men and mighty Troy.*
Out of her lone and close-veil'd chambers she,
    Curtain'd with gorgeous tapestry,
Reckless, spread out her flying sail
    To the giant Zephyr's gale.
The many hero-hunters on her track,
Each his broad shield upon his back,
Followed the vanishing dimpling of her oars
To Simois' leaf-embowered shores;
    So rapid and so far,
Even to the outburst of that sanguinary war.

ANTISTROPHE.

To Ilion in beauty came
The wedded mischief! of her name
The wrath of the great Gods on high
Fulfilled the awful augury;

* The play on Ἑλένα, ἑλέναος, ἑλανδρός, ἑλέπτολις—the *taker* of ships, men, and cities—is of course untranslateable. The Greeks were fond of these *jeux de mots*, even in their most serious moods. Milton ventured to imitate them. I did not think it right therefore altogether to avoid the allusion, though of itself bare and unmeaning. I have ventured on *destroy* and *Troy:* the *Hell* of ships, men, and cities would have been too strong.

The hoarded vengeance long preparing
For that deed of guilty daring :
Dishonour of the stranger-welcoming board,
  And Jove, the Hospitable God and lord.
The brothers of the house, that princely throng,
  With the glad hymenean song,
  Hymned the eve of that bright wedding-day.
  That hymn unlearned, a sadder lay
Shall Priam's ancient city chant anon—
The many-voiced wail and moan,
In evil hour o'er Paris led
To that disastrous bridal-bed :
  Foredoomed t' endure the flood
For years poured wasteful of her citizens' blood.

STROPHE 2.

That king, within his palace nurst
The dangerous lion cub, at first
Taking his bland and blameless feast
Of innocent milk from the full breast ;
Gentle, with whom a child might toy ;
He was the old man's sport and joy ;
Oft in their arms, tired out with play,
Like to a new-born babe he lay,
Or fondly fawning would he stand
And hungry licked his food from the caressing hand.

ANTISTROPHE 2.

Time passes—quickly he displays
His ruthless kind's blood-thirsting ways:
And this was the return he made,
Thus the fond fostering care repaid :
Upon the innocent flocks to feast
Insatiate, an unbidden guest.
And all the house reeks thick with blood.
The unresisting servants stood
Shuddering before th' unconquered beast,
Heaven willed, so in that house was nursed fell Ate's
    priest.

STROPHE 3.

Too soon in Troy, her coming seemed to be
Like gentle calm over the waveless sea ;
She stood, an image of bright wealth untold.
   Oblique from her soft eye the dart
   Preyed sweetly on the inmost heart,
Making love's flower its tenderest bloom unfold.
So changing with the changing hours
   That wedlock brought her to a bitter end,
   A cruel sister, and a cruel friend,
To Priam's daughters in their chamber bowers :
   By Hospitable Jove sent in his ire,
No tender bride, rather a Fury dark and dire.

ANTISTROPHE 3.

There is 'mong men a proverb wise and old :
Enormous wealth, to its full height uproll'd,
Its haughty race will ever propagate,
    Childless and heirless 'twill not die ;
    Merciless unglutted misery
Falls on its doomed descendants soon or late.
I stand not in the thought alone,
    That overweening wickedness will yet
    High overweening wickedness beget.
Be that eternal truth to some unknown ;
    While in the mansions of the just, from age
To age, goes down of bliss the unbroken heritage.

STROPHE 4.

For godless pride does not with years decay,
    And still of godless pride will bring
    A new, an everlasting spring
On her predestined day ;
And still shall gorged Satiety conspire,
    With that dread dæmon unsubdued,
High-handed and unholy Hardihood,
Each of them hideous as his sire :
And o'er the stately palace shall let fall
    Ate's funereal pall.

ANTISTROPHE 4.

But Justice, underneath the cottage roof,
   Smoke-darkened, evermore hath shone,
   Where decent life flows peaceful on.
With backward eye, aloof
Turning, she condescends not to behold
   The palace sprinkled o'er with gold,
And foulness on the deep attainted hands;
Still in her holiness she stands;
No worshipper of wealth's ill-lauded power
   Waits calmly her last hour.

AGAMEMNON *enters.*

CHORUS.

Hail, king of Atreus' race renowned,
Who Troy hast levelled with the ground!
How to address thee—how adore;
Nor with exceeding praise run o'er,
Nor turning short, pass by too light
The mark and standard of thy might.
Most men do justice' law transgress,
Being than seeming honouring less.
And every one is prompt of will
To groan over another's ill;
So grief its prudent temperance keep,
Nor sink into the heart too deep,

As with mock sympathy to guile,
Force on the face the unwilling smile.
Who knows his sheep, the shepherd good,
The eye of man will ne'er delude,
Seeking his friend's blind heart to move
With a faint, thin, and watery love.
  Thou when, for sake of Helen lost,
Thou didst array that mighty host,
Wert written (nought may I disguise),
Within my books as most unwise,
Handling with impulse rash and blind
The helm of thy misguided mind.
But no light-minded counsellor now
To that bold army seemest thou—
The sagest and the truest friend,
Who hast brought their toils to this proud end.
For evermore will Time reveal
  Those who with prescient judgment wise,
  Nor missing golden opportunities,
Administer for public good the public weal.

AGAMEMNON.

'Tis meet that Argos and my country's Gods
First I salute, gracious accomplices
In my return, and the just vengeance wrought
On Priam's city. The great Gods the cause
Judge not from pleaders' subtle rhetoric,
But cast their suffrage-balls with one consent

Into the bloody urn, that doomed to ruin
Ilion, to one wide slaughter all her sons;
And in the opposite urn was only Hope
Wild-grasping with her clenched and unfilled hands.
 Now captive Troy is one vast cloud of smoke;
Howls Ate's hurricane, the dying embers
Steam up with the fat reek of burning riches.
For this our unforgetting thanks we pay
To the great Gods, since we our hunters' toils
With one wide sweep have o'er the city cast.
The Argive dragon, for that woman's sake,
Hath utterly razed to earth once famous Troy.
Foaled by the fatal horse, the shielded host,
At the Pleiads' setting, leaped terrific forth;
The roaring lion rampant o'er the towers
Sprang, glutting his fierce maw with kingly blood.
 Such is my prelude to the immortal Gods,
But for the rest my thoughts are as your thoughts.
The same aver I, and do fully assent.
Few, few are born with that great gift, to hail
Unenvying their friends' prosperity.
Envy, slow poison gnawing at the heart
Doubles the anguish of the man diseased;
By his own woes weighed heavily down, he groans
Gazing at the happiness before his doors.
From sad experience of mankind I speak,
To human life holding the mirror up.
Even as the shadow of a shade I saw

Those that once seemed my dearest, best of friends.
Only Ulysses, who against his will
Set sail, my one true yokemate, by my side
Ran in the harness of the battle-car.
But speak I of the living or the dead,
Passes, alas! my knowledge.

       For the city
And for our Gods holding our festal games
In full assembly, take we counsel now;
Take counsel how what now stands well may stand
Unshaken even unto the end of time;
And wheresoe'er needs healing remedy,
By cautery or incision, skilful and keen,
We will divert the growing slow disease.

 Enter we now our palace' hallowed hearths,
Our Gods propitiated, who to far lands
Sent us, and brought us back; and Victory,
Who hath tracked our steps, abide with us for ever!

CLYTEMNESTRA *enters.*

CLYTEMNESTRA.

Men! citizens! Elders of Argos' state!
I blush not in your presence to pour forth
All a wife's fondness for her lord beloved;
For timorous bashfulness soon dies away
Before familiar faces. Not from others
Learning, but only from mine own sad knowledge

Will I describe my solitary life,
While he was far away under Troy's walls.
And first, what monstrous misery to sit,
A desolate woman in a lonely house!
No man in the wide palace, listening still
To rumours strange, confused, and contrary.
First comes a melancholy messenger,
Another then, with tidings worse and worse,
Shrieking their dreary tale through the lone chambers
And thus poured down the news upon the house—
" The wounded man had had his body pierced
With gaping holes as many as in a net ;"
Then " he was dead," so swelled and grew the tale,
" A second triple-bodied Geryon he
(Of Geryon* I speak, living on earth
Not Geryon in the infernal realms below)—
Three deaths had suffered in his threefold form,
And thence been wrapped in a winding-sheet of earth.
While these conflicting rumours thronged around,
Others the desperate halter round my neck,
By which I hung, loosening with friendly hand,
Brought me with gentle violence back to life.

* I cannot but point out what seems to me the bearing of this most masterly touch. Clytemnestra, in her artful declamation, would seem seized with a fit of holy reticence. She will allude only to Geryon alive, not as the enemy of the gods in hell. She avoids the ill-omened comparison of Agamemnon to Geryon in hell.
Throughout—
" Methinks the lady doth protest too much."

And all the while our boy, as had been meet—
He, seal and pledge of our affianced troth—
Orestes, was not by me.   Marvel not
That child, the Phocian Strophius, once our foe,
Now our close friend, nurses within his palace.
He the dark choice of evil that lay before me
Showed, prophet-like—thy peril 'neath Troy's walls,
Or democratic anarchy at home,
The senate overthrown, and the mad people,
As wont with men, trampling upon the fallen.
Such was the warning—warning that deceived not.
To me the gushing fountains of my tears
Were utterly dried up, no drop would fall.
Mine eyes grew dim upon my late-sought bed,
Weeping, and watching the neglected lamps
Paling their feebler light ; and in my dreams
I woke at the shrill buzzing of the gnats ;
I saw thee suffering woes more long and sad
Than could be crowded in my hours of sleep.

 I, that have borne all this with soul unblenched,
May now address my lord in happier phrase.
Thou, watchdog of the unattainted fold !
The main-stay that secures the straining ship !
The firm-based pillar, bearing the lofty roof !
The only son to childless father born !
Land by the lost despairing sailor seen !
Day beaming beautiful after fierce storms !
Cool fountain to the thirsty traveller !

And, oh! what bliss to be delivered thus
From the hard bondage of necessity.
None grudge us now our joy! For woe enough
We have endured.
     And now, O most beloved,
Alight thou from thy chariot.
       Stay, nor set
On the bare earth, O King, thy hallowed foot;
That which hath trampled upon ruined Troy.
Why tarry ye, my damsels? 'Tis your office
To strew the path with gorgeous carpetings;
Like purple pavement rich be all his way;
That justice to his house may lead him in—
The house he little dreamed of.* All the rest
Leave to my care, that may not sleep. So please
The Gods, what's justly destined shall be done.

AGAMEMNON.

Daughter of Leda, guardian of mine house!
Of my long absence thou hast spoken well,
But hast been somewhat lavish of thy praise.
Praise in due measure and discreet is well,
Yet may that guerdon come from others best.
Treat me not like a soft and delicate woman,

---

* Ἐς δῶμ' ἄελπτον. I have endeavoured faintly to preserve the untranslateable ambiguity, the terrible ambiguity, of the word ἄελπτον. What to Agamemnon seems to mean only his unhoped-for return, to the spectator hints at the unexpected reception he is to meet with.

Nor, gazing open-mouthed, grovelling on earth
Like a barbarian, raise discordant cry;
Nor, strewing with bright tapestries my way,
Make me an envy to all-jealous Heaven.
These are the proud prerogatives of the Gods;
That mortal thus should walk on rich embroideries
Beseems not: do it I cannot without awe.
As a man, honour me, not as a God!
Though she wipe not her feet on carpetings,
Nor variegated garments fine, Fame lifts
High her clear voice. To be of humble mind
Is God's best gift. Blessed is only he
Who in unbroken happiness ends his days.
Still may I prosper, thus not overbold.

CLYTEMNESTRA.

Say ye not so; nor cross my purpose thus.

AGAMEMNON.

Think not that I will change my fixed resolve.

CLYTEMNESTRA.

Hast thou thus sworn in awe of the great Gods?

AGAMEMNON.

If man e'er knew his purpose, know I mine.

CLYTEMNESTRA.

Had Priam conquered, what had Priam done?

AGAMEMNON.

He would have trod on gorgeous carpetings.

CLYTEMNESTRA.

So, cower not thou before the blame of men.

AGAMEMNON.

The people's voice bears with it mighty power.

CLYTEMNESTRA.

He that's not envied never is admired.

AGAMEMNON.

'Tis not a woman's part to love a fray.

CLYTEMNESTRA.

The prosperous should condescend to yield.

AGAMEMNON.

Wilt thou be conqueress in this gentle strife?

CLYTEMNESTRA.

Be thou persuaded, yield of thine own free will!

AGAMEMNON.

If thou wilt have it so, then let some slave
Loose instantly the sandals from my feet,

Lest some dread God with jealous eye behold me
Walking like them upon the sea-dipt purple.
It were great shame to pamper one's own body,
Trampling on riches with proud prodigal feet,
And tapestries with untold silver bought.
So much for this.
     But thou this stranger maid
Lead in with courteous welcome. The high Gods
On him who rules his slaves with gentleness
Look gracious: for to bear the yoke of slavery
Is a sore trial to the struggling will.
And she, of our rich spoils the chosen flower,
The army's precious gift, follows me here.
And since to yield to thee I am compelled,
Walking on purple, enter I the palace.

CLYTEMNESTRA.

Who shall go quench the prodigal sea, that still
Teems with bright purple, worth its weight in silver,
The ever-fresh and never-fading dye
That steeps our robes in everlasting colours?
Of these, O king, our house hath ample store—
Our house that knows not vulgar poverty.
Of many as rich the trampling in the dust
I would have vowed, if the oracular shrine,
At which I knelt, had uttered such decree,
Working the ransom for thy precious life.

Be the root sound, upsprings the full-leaved tree,
Offering cool shade beneath the dog-star heat.
So as thou cam'st to the domestic hearth,
'Twas as a sunny warmth in winter time,
When Jove the sharp grape ripens to rich wine:
And a delicious freshness fills the house,
The prime of men moving through the long chambers.
 Jove! Jove! that all things perfectest, my prayers
Bring to perfection! to perfection bring
What thou hast yet to do! Be this thy care.

CHORUS.

STROPHE 1.

Why, why for evermore,
 With irresistible control,
 Doth still the indwelling Terror hover o'er
  My portent-haunted soul?
Why doth the unbought, unbidden song
Its dark prophetic descant still prolong?
Why does not bold Assurance, doubly sure,
 Scattering with orient light
 The dim-seen dreams of night,
Take its firm seat upon my bosom's throne?
 Long of that time the youth hath past,
  Since on the sands that sea-borne host
 From their tall prows their anchors cast,
  Bound for far Ilion's coast.

ANTISTROPHE 1.

I've seen them homeward come,
   Mine own glad witness I,
  Yet not the less that hymn of unblest gloom,
   Not to the sweet lyre's harmony,
But to the Erynnys' wild and wailing din,
Chants, self-inspired, the secret soul within.
My bowels yearn, not vainly, nor for nought
   (All hope is gone and lost),
   And in wild whirlpools tost,
O'er doom to be fulfilled broods with sad thought
   My restless eddying heart!
    But oh! of all this boded ill,
  I pray the Gods, at least some scanty part
   May ne'er the Fates fulfil.

STROPHE 2.

Wealth in its full excess still swells
  Beyond all bound, insatiate;
  By a thin party-wall but separate,
'Neath the same roof, Disease, close neighbour,
    dwells.
  Still Fate, on the unseen breakers dark,
  Dashes the proud sea-going bark.
The crew, as from well-balanced sling,
  From off the overladen deck
The heavy burden of their riches fling.

Yet, with calamity o'erfull,
   Sinks not at once the whole strong hull ;
Nor is the noble ship an utter wreck.
   With blessing from above,
   Still ample-handed Jove
Commands the teeming furrows to repair
The slow disease of the famine-stricken year.

ANTISTROPHE 2.

But who, with charm of potent sound
   Or magic spell, can summon back
   The human blood, all curdling thick and black,
Once shed and drunk up by the thirsty ground ?
   Jove checked the pride of the overwise
   Who made the dead to life arise ;
For if another higher fate
   Rebuke the fate revealed to me,
Mine heart would my slow tongue anticipate ;
   And though forbid to utter more,
   Its weary load would all outpour,
Its dismal burthen of dark prophecy.
   In frenzied solitude
   Still silent would it brood,
Nor hope the inextricable clue to unwind,
Though burn the living fire in the distracted mind.

CLYTEMNESTRA, CASSANDRA.

CLYTEMNESTRA.

Get thee within, Cassandra!—thee I mean—
Since Jove, not in his wrath, hath given to thee,
With many another slave, to gather round
The lavers of our house, and take your stand
By th' altar of our treasure-guarding god.
Come down, then, from the chariot: look not proud!
'Tis said that even Alcmena's son endured,
Sold as a bond-slave, forced to stoop to the yoke.
If fortune, then, to this necessity
Hath bowed thee down, 'tis a great boon to serve
The high-born lords of old ancestral wealth.
The upstarts, that have reaped unhoped-for riches,
Are cruel to their slaves beyond all measure.
Here thou wilt have what rule and custom give.

CHORUS.

Clearly she speaks, and now has ceased to speak;
But thou, poor captive in the toils of fate!
Be well persuaded, if I may persuade thee;
But haply no persuasion will prevail.

CLYTEMNESTRA.

If, like a chattering swallow, she speaks not
Some strange barbarian tongue, I shall persuade her
With words that commune with the mind within.

CHORUS.

Submit! the queen speaks what is best for thee.
Obey, and from thy chariot-seat dismount.

CLYTEMNESTRA.

I have no time to waste here at the gates.
Already in the central palace hall
The sheep stand by the sacrificial fire;
A blessing far beyond our utmost hopes!
Thou, if wilt do as I command, delay not;
But if thou understand'st not, make a sign
Instead of speech, with thy barbarian hands.

CHORUS.

The stranger seems some clear interpreter
To need, she looks a wild beast newly caught.

CLYTEMNESTRA.

She raves, or listens to some evil spirit;
Who, having left but now a new-sacked city,
Comes here, and champs the bit; she will not yield
Till she hath foamed away her strength in blood.
To a waste of words I will no more demean me.

      [CLYTEMNESTRA *retires*.

CHORUS.

But I have more of pity than of wrath.
Come, sad one, yield! leaving the empty car,
Acquaint thee with necessity's hard yoke.

CASSANDRA.

Alas! alas! oh woe, oh woe!
    Apollo! O Apollo!

CHORUS.

Why that alas! alas! to Phœbus sent?
No God is he that hears the shrill lament.

CASSANDRA.

Alas! alas! oh woe, oh woe!
    Apollo! O Apollo!

CHORUS.

Still to the God thy voice ill-omened cries,
Who listens not to mortal agonies.

CASSANDRA.

Apollo! Apollo!
My guide, my deity!
Once more, destroyer, thou destroyest me!

CHORUS.

Of her own woes her prophet-accents rave,
And still the God, the God inspires the slave.

CASSANDRA.

Apollo! Apollo!
My guide, my deity!
Whither? to what dread dwelling lead'st thou me?

CHORUS.

The house of Atreus' son! Dost not perceive?
Trust in my words, which may not, maid, deceive.

CASSANDRA.

Dwelling accurst of God!
    Dark home of murder and infanticide!
The lord lies slaughtered in that drear abode,
    And the dank floor with bloody dew is dyed.

CHORUS.

Wondrous and strange! like to the keenest hound
The prophet-slave the scent of blood hath found.

CASSANDRA.

Woe! woe! the witnesses of murder rise!
I hear the slaughtered infants' wailing cries!
    I see the miserable sire at feast
    Upon his mangled children's breast.

CHORUS.

Well have we heard of old thy prophet-name;
Yet needs no prophet of what's known to fame.

CASSANDRA.

Now, now a deed they meditate,
    The irremediable deed of fate;

He who might the stroke delay
The strength of the doomed house, is far away.

CHORUS.

I know not now what direful deed she sings;
The first I knew—of that all Argos rings.

CASSANDRA.

Wretch! wretch! and darest thou do the deed—
Thy lord, the partner of thy bed?
Now, now the bath, I see them tend;
I may not, dare not, see the end.
Soon, soon it comes; I see them stand,
Hand already linked in hand.

CHORUS.

Darker and darker now she raves along,
And wrapt in riddles flows the boding song.

CASSANDRA.

Alas! alas! more horrors yet!
God of death! I see thy net;
The murderess-wife the net hath spread!
Let that dark sisterhood,
The Furies, all insatiate of blood,
Howl for the victim, howl to death by stoning led.*

---

* This seems to refer to the fate of Clytemnestra.

CHORUS.

To what fell power in the drear house of woe,
    Wilt thou we shriek aloud our frantic strain?
Nor light, nor comfort, her dark accents show.
    To my heart the yellow blood-drop flows;
As when the dying on the battle-plain
    Their setting days in mortal anguish close.
Seest thou now some stroke of fate?

CASSANDRA.

Away, away, from his fell mate,
    Lead the lordly bull away;
Entangled in his fraudful vest,
Lo now they strike the black-horned beast,
    And in the bath the mangled corpse they lay.

CHORUS.

I do not boast divining skill,
Yet well I bode some coming ill.
For when did mystic oracle
Tidings of good delight to tell?
From prophets' many-worded songs we hear
Only the fateful strains of fear.

CASSANDRA.

Alas! alas! for myself I fear
    Mine own death hour of agony!

Oh, wherefore do ye lead me here ?
  Oh, wherefore, but with him to die ?

CHORUS.

Oh, thou art frantic, heaven-struck, all thy cry
Strange inharmonious harmony ;
Thus aye incessant pours her tale.
  (For still the longer that she lives,
    More young and fresh her grief revives.)
Itys! Itys! her everlasting wail,
The yellow nightingale.

CASSANDRA.

O happy Philomel! kind heaven
To her a winged form hath given,
A long blest life without a tear.
I, wretched I, must fall by the two-edged spear.

CHORUS.

Why heaven-struck, heaping ill on ill,
  Pour'st thou thy frantic sorrows vain ?
Why shrieks thy voice, ill-omened still,
  Its awful burthen in awakening strain ?
Why roams thy sad prophetic song
Only the paths of grief along ?

CASSANDRA.

Woe, Paris, woe! for thy fatal bridal-bed !
  Woe for Scamander's stream ! of yore

On that delightful shore,
My joyous youth I led.
   By Acheron and Cocytus slow,
   Now my prophet strains must flow.

CHORUS.

Why speak'st thou thus so plain and clear,
   An infant might thy meaning know.
Deep am I pierced by the sharp fang of fear,
   While sounds thy soft lament of woe,
Which breaks the heart to hear.

CASSANDRA.

   Alas! alas!
For the lost city's long and weary toil,
My father's vain and frequent hecatomb,
   His streams of sacrificial blood,
That nought availed t' avert that city's doom.
   And I, with soul fired by the God,
Must lie and perish on a foreign soil.

CHORUS.

Dark, dark as ever! last as first!
By what dread dæmon art thou curst,
That lies upon thy soul with crushing weight,
Making thee sing of woe, and death, and fate?
   I know not yet the worst.

CASSANDRA.

And now no longer the dark oracle,
Like a young bride, from out her close-wrapt veil
Looks forth, but in bright day it breaks abroad
In splendour like the dawn.   How billow-like,
Woe rolls on woe, each heavier than the last,
In the light of heaven.
      Of riddles now no more!
Bear ye me witness with how keen a scent
I've tracked the trail of those dread deeds of old.
Never shall quit that roof the direful choir,
Concordant, not harmonious, whose drear tone
Ne'er breathed of good.   Yea, and within yon palace,
Emboldened by his draughts of human blood,
The ill-bidden God of revels hold his state
Beside his kindred Furies.   All at once
Close seated round those walls accurst, they hymn
That primal guilt of all, the bed of incest,
A brother mounting on a brother's couch.
Err I? or strike the white, an archeress true?
Or am I a false wandering witch, that knocks
At any door?   Bear witness ye, make oath
How well I know that house's ancient sins.

CHORUS.

What help in oaths, however deeply sworn?
But much I marvel, how, far beyond sea,

Nursed in a foreign city, foreign tongue,
Thou speak'st of all things as if native here.

CASSANDRA.

Prophet Apollo made this office mine.

CHORUS.

What! was the God inflamed with fond desire?

CASSANDRA.

Till now I was ashamed to speak of this.

CHORUS.

Blest natures are not least to softness prone.

CASSANDRA.

He was my foe, yet full of breathing kindness.

CHORUS.

What! met ye in the gentle strife of love?

CASSANDRA.

By feigned consent great Loxias I deceived.

CHORUS.

Already gifted with divining skill?

CASSANDRA.

Already to the city boding woe.

CHORUS.

'Scap'st thou uninjured stern Apollo's wrath?

CASSANDRA.

None would believe my warnings: there I failed.

CHORUS.

Alas! to me thou seem'st to bode too truly.

CASSANDRA.

Alas! alas! woe upon woe!
The dire awakening toil of prophecy
Whirls and distracts my soul with prelude dread.
See, see ye not upon yon palace roofs
Like shapes in dreams, they stand and jibber there,
The children murdered by their nearest kin?
Lo there they are, in their full-laden hands
Entrails and bowels, horrible food, on which
Their fathers have been feasting. For these deeds
A terrible vengeance does the unvaliant lion
That rolls about on his incestuous bed
Prepare 'gainst him who on the threshold stands—
My master—for a slave I needs must be.
He, the fleet's captain, conqueror of Troy,
Observes not with what bland and glozing words,
What seeming soul serene, like some dark Fate,
That she-wolf welcomes him in evil hour.

Such height of impious daring hers! a woman
The murderer of a man! What shall I call
The unloveable monster? Amphisbæna dire,
Or Scylla on the rocks, the mariner's ruin,
Mother of hell and priestess! 'gainst her kin
Breathing implacable relentless war.
How, as a conqueror in the thick of battle,
Shrieked she, the all-daring woman! the while
Rejoicing in his homeward safe return.
If things like these win not belief, what then?
What comes will come, and thou, even in this presence,
Ere long wilt vouch me a true prophetess.

CHORUS.

That Thyestean feast of infants' flesh
I understood, and shuddered, horror-struck;
I heard those awful truths, not idly guess'd.
For thy last words, I wander from the course.

CASSANDRA.

I say thou shalt behold Atrides' doom.

CHORUS.

Wild woman, lull thy lips to reverent silence.

CASSANDRA.

There's no physician can unspell my words.

CHORUS.

Not if it must be.   Grant, Heaven, that it be not!

CASSANDRA.

'Tis thine to pray, but it is theirs to murder.

CHORUS.

And who is he to accomplish this dark crime?

CASSANDRA.

Have ye so look'd askance on my dread oracles?

CHORUS.

By what decree 'tis to be done I see not.

CASSANDRA.

And yet thou knowest well the Grecian tongue.

CHORUS.

The Gods' words must come true!   How, guess I not.

CASSANDRA.

Away! the fire! the fire! it leaps on me!
Alas, alas! Apollo! ah me! me!
She, the two-footed lioness, who sleeps
With the base wolf in her adulterous bed
(And he the kingly lion far away),

F

Shall slay me, wretched me! Brewing her poison,
She makes me an ingredient of her wrath;
Whetting against her lord her bloody sword,
My presence here she boasts that she avenges.
 Why wear I these in mockery of myself—
The sceptre, on my head the prophet-garlands?
Off, off! ye all shall perish ere I perish!
Down with you! down to the dust—thus I requite you!
Adorn, instead of me, some other wretch!
Lo! lo! Apollo's self hath stripp'd from me
My robes prophetic! made a show of me
In these once-hallowed trappings; laughed to scorn
By friends, by foes—dissentient none. How vain!
No doubt, in baser and more bitter scorn,
A strolling witch, a juggler, I had been call'd—
Beggar, wretch, starveling! and for thee I bore it.
Prophet! thou hast undone thy prophetess,
And hither leadest her to shameful death.
For the altar of my sire the block awaits me,*
Where I shall be cut down, with my hot blood
Spouting—sad victim.
 Yet I shall not die
Of the great Gods unhonoured, unappeased.
He comes, in his due time the Avenger comes,

---

* Virgil on the death of Priam—
 "Hoc dicens altaria ad ipsa
 Traxit, et in multo lapsantem sanguine nati," etc.
  ÆNEID, ii. 550.

The matricidal son, for his sire's blood
Exactor of the awful penalty.
Lo, he comes back, a vagrant exile long,
To his own land a stranger, to build up
The topmost cornice-stone of guilt and fate;
For by the Gods a mighty oath is sworn
That he shall come to lift, in the face of heaven,
His father's corpse, that grovels now supine.

  But what do I, a stranger, moaning here,
Since I have seen but now proud Ilion
Fall'n as it fell, and its inhabitants
All perishing by the judgment of the Gods?
I'll do it, I'll do it—I will endure to die;
And you I do invoke, ye gates of Hell,
That I encounter but one mortal stroke;
So, my blood ebbing out with gentle flow,
Without a struggle I may close mine eyes.

CHORUS.

O woefullest of women, wise as woeful!
Thy speech hath wander'd far. But if in truth
Thou dost foresee thy death, why, like a heifer,
God-driven, to the altar dost thou boldly tread?

CASSANDRA.

There's no escape. What gain I by delay?

CHORUS.

Who lingers still wins something by delay.

CASSANDRA.

My day is come; flight were but little gain.

CHORUS.

Thou'lt suffer more by being overbold.

CASSANDRA.

A glorious death is mortals' noblest grace.

CHORUS.

The happy speak not thus—That ne'er was heard.

CASSANDRA.

Oh! oh! my father! Oh thy valiant sons!

CHORUS.

How now! what terror makes thee thus start back?

CASSANDRA.

Foh! foh!

CHORUS.

Why this foh, foh! unless thou art sick at heart?

CASSANDRA.

Foh! how the house smells with the reek of blood!

CHORUS.

'Tis but the smell of the sacrificial fires!

CASSANDRA.

It is the vapour oozing from a tomb.

CHORUS.

Sooth, 'tis no smell of Syrian incense rich.

CASSANDRA.

Well, then, I go to shriek throughout the palace
Mine own and Agamemnon's bloody fate.
Enough of life! enough! Strangers! good strangers!
I am not screaming like a timorous bird
That hides itself behind the bush, in vain!
To one about to die, bear ye this witness!
When that a woman dies for me a woman!
A man ill-wedded for a murdered man!
Remember well the expiring stranger's words.

CHORUS.

Sad one! I pity thy foreboded fate.

CASSANDRA.

Yet once more would I speak in sober speech,
Or ere I utter mine own funeral wail.
And thee do I conjure, all-seeing Sun!
Gazing upon thy light for the last time;
Even fate as terrible, as dire as this,
May my avengers on my murderers wreak;

On both the murderers of a dying slave,
An easy victim in their mastering hand!
Oh, our poor mortal state! the happiest
A shadow turns to grief—the unfortunate!
A wet sponge with one touch washes all out
The picture: far more pitiable these.

      [*Enters the palace.*

CHORUS.

Of the gifts that from good fortune fall
Insatiate still are mortals all;
At whom all fingers point, the great
Who warns men from his palace gate,
And says, "Thou mayst not enter here;"
To him, the monarch standing near,
Did the blest Gods the boon bestow,
Old Priam's city to o'erthrow.
Of all the Gods we saw him come
Most honoured to his native home.
But if the forfeit he repays,
For the foul crimes of ancient days,
And vengeance for the olden dead,
Be heaped on his devoted head;
What mortal would not make his prayer
That he were born beneath a lowlier star?

AGAMEMNON (*within*).

Woe's me, I'm stabbed! stabbed with a mortal blow!

CHORUS 1.

Silence! who is he that's shouting—stricken by a mortal stroke?

AGAMEMNON.

Woe's me! woe's me! again; another blow.

CHORUS 2.

From the groaning of the monarch—seems it that the deed is done.

CHORUS 3.

Let us join in instant counsel—what were safest to be done.

CHORUS 4.

My voice is that we raise a general cry,
Summoning all Argos to the palace here.

CHORUS 5.

Mine that we break at once into the palace,
And seize the assassin with his reeking blade.

CHORUS 6.

The same say I; what's to be done do quickly;
This is no time for tardy dallying.

CHORUS 7.

'Tis clear as day—'Tis the first step to slavery,
The signal for a bloody tyranny.

CHORUS 8.

What! loitering still! haste, trample down delay,
The hand of the avenger must not sleep.

CHORUS 9.

I know not what t' advise! were it not best
'Gainst him take counsel who hath done the deed.

CHORUS 10.

I'm of your mind; I know not with our cries
How we can raise again the dead to life.

CHORUS 11.

What! shall we yield, and drag out our base lives
'Neath chiefs who so disgrace our noble house.

CHORUS 12.

It is not to be borne, better were death:
Nobler to die, than live under a tyrant.

CHORUS 13.

But where our proofs? but from the groans we heard
Conclude we surely that the man is dead.

CHORUS 14.

We must have certain knowledge of the deed
Of which we speak. To guess is not to know.

CHORUS.

On all sides presses on me the same thought,
We must know well, how 'tis with Atreus' son.

CLYTEMNESTRA.

Erewhile I spake words suited to the time;
Of opposite and contrary import now
Unblushing do I speak. His enemies
Who treats as enemies, friends though they seem,
Does not build up the enveloping toils of death
Only so high that they may be o'erleaped.
This is no unpremeditated strife:
Over this ancient feud I have brooded long,
That the slow time at length hath brought to pass.
Here stand I, as I smote.* 'Twas I that slew him!
Thus, thus I did it! Nought will I deny!
That he could nor defend himself, nor 'scape.
As round the fish the inextricable net
Closes, in his rich garments' fatal wealth
I wrapt him. Then once, twice, I smote him home.
Twice groaned he, then stretched out his failing limbs;
And as he lay I added a third blow;
And unto Hades, the dark god below,

---

* Here, as Otfried Müller has shown (*Æschylos Eumeniden*, pp. 73, 103), the scene opened, and disclosed the bath-chamber, in the interior of the palace. Clytemnestra appeared standing over the dead body of Agamemnon.

Warden of the dead, made my thanksgiving vow
So, fallen thus, he breathed out his proud life,
And spouted forth such a quick rush of blood,

It splashed me o'er with its black gory dew.
Yet not the less rejoiced I, than the flower
Within the pregnant folds of its sweet cup
Rejoices in the dropping dews of heaven.
Being as it is, ye Argive elders all,
If that ye too feel joy, rejoice with me,
And I protest that were it meet to make
Libations for the dead, 'tis I would make them:
For all that's done is just—is more than just.
He that hath filled the chalice of this house
With cursing and with woe, on his return
Himself should drink it to the very dregs.

CHORUS.

We are amazed at thy audacious tongue,
Thus glorying o'er thy murdered husband's corpse.

CLYTEMNESTRA.

Ye try me as a woman void of sense;
As to experienced men, I speak to you,
With heart that knows not fear. Praise me, or blame me,
'Tis one to me. He that lies here a corpse
Is Agamemnon, is my husband—dead
Even by mine hand, the righteous artisan
Of this great work of death. So let it be.

CHORUS.

Woman! what evil food, earth-nurst,
   Hath maddened thee, what venomous potion
     From the low depths of the salt ocean,
To this dire sacrifice accurst
   By the universal voice of men?
     Thou hast cast him off,
     Thou hast cut him off;
  And with one voice we sentence thee
  An outcast from this realm to be,
The unreconciled hate of every citizen.

CLYTEMNESTRA.

Ye sentence me to eternal banishment,
The citizens' hate—the curses of the people.

Yet not one word gainst this man did ye speak.
He, rating her no more than a young lamb
Chosen from all his woolly-fleeced flock,
Sacrificed his own child—his child and mine—
Most precious travail of my womb, a charm
To lull the adverse Thracian winds to rest.
Should ye not have driven out this cruel man
To expiate the deep stain of his guilt?
For judgment on my deeds, ye sit as judges
Harsh and unrighteous. Yet this do I say:
Threaten me, I will meet your threats with threats!
Get ye the victory o'er me if you can!
But if the Gods shall otherwise decree,
Old men! ye'll learn in time to be more wise.

CHORUS.

Woman, thou art haughty-souled,
With words beyond all boldness bold;
And thy mind is maddening yet,
With the gore distilling wet:
An unavenged blood-drop lies
Reddening in thine angry eyes;
Still, with all thy friends away,
Blow for blow wilt thou repay.

CLYTEMNESTRA.

And now hear ye my stern, my solemn oath :—
By Justice, the avenger of my child;

By Atê, by Erynnys, at whose shrine
I have offered up this man, slain by mine hand!
I look not in the house of fear to dwell,
So long as on my hearth kindles his fire
Ægisthus, as of old my constant friend:
He to my daring is no slender shield.
Low lies the man who hath done shameful wrong
To me his wife; he, once the dear delight
Of the fair Chryseid, 'neath the walls of Troy;
And her his captive, her his prophetess,
The sharer of his bed, his soothsayer,
His faithful consort on his couch of sleep,
And on the deck, under the groaning masts.
For this these two have paid the rightful price—
He as ye see him; she, like the sweet swan,
Singing her farewell song, her own sad dirge,
Lies here, his paramour, the delicate morsel,
Intruded here, where I should feast alone.

SEMICHORUS.

Oh, that some sudden fate, not with slow anguish,
Nor making long on the sick-bed to languish,
Now that is gone our gracious lord and king,
To me sweet everlasting sleep would bring.
What hath he borne through her, his wife,
By her relentless hand bereft of life!

CHORUS.

Helen! O Helen! O thou frantic one!
    Through thee, through thee alone,
How many noble lives have been o'erthrown
    Under the walls of Troy?

SEMICHORUS.

And now in this sad hour
    Thou'st nipped that flower of perfect grace—
That ne'er-forgotten flower—
    Through blood that nought can e'er efface.
Her in that house the unsubdued strife,
The bane of the great lord, hate of the jealous wife.

CLYTEMNESTRA.

No! pray not ye for instant fate,
Under your sorrows' crushing weight;
Nor heap your wrath on Helen's head,
As the sole murderess of the dead;
As she alone, of many Greeks laid low
The Fate, had wrought all this unmeasured woe.

SEMICHORUS.

    Dæmon, who dost ever fall
    On the proud Tantalid hall?
    As thy dire presence haunted erst,
    All down that double line accurst;

On these twain women so may come
In equal share that awful doom—
The doom that eats my wretched heart away.
Like some hoarse raven o'er her prey,
Stands she, and o'er that corpse all desolate
Hymns with shrill shriek the tuneless hymn of fate.

CHORUS.

*   *   *
*   *   *

SEMICHORUS.

*   *   *

CLYTEMNESTRA.

Aye, now in thy wild raving word
Some sense, some meaning may be heard.
Well that thrice-monstrous Dæmon now,
That haunts this house, invokest thou!
From him that foul blood-lapping thirst
Is in their greedy bowels nurst.
   Ere the old grief is o'er,
     Gushes anew the unexhausted gore.

SEMICHORUS.

And dar'st thou name that Dæmon dread,
Whose wrath hangs heavy o'er the head
Of each of that predestined line;
A name, the omen and the sign

Of endless and insatiate misery.
Alas! alas! from Jove on high,
Does that avenging Dæmon come—
Jove, lord and arbiter of doom;
The author and the cause of all
To mortal man that can befall:
For whatsoe'er on earth is done
Is from the hand of Jove alone.

CHORUS.

Alas! alas!
My king! my king! how shall I mourn for thee?
How my fond heart speak all its agony?
There liest thou; thy cold corpse around
The subtle spider's web is wound;
Thy noble life thou didst outbreathe
By a most impious and unholy death.

SEMICHORUS.

Woe's me! woe's me! on that base bed,
Unseemly for thy kingly head,
Thou liest, by fraud to death trepanned
By that two-edged axe held in that murderous hand.

CLYTEMNESTRA.

And dar'st thou say the deed was mine?
Ill does thy erring speech divine.

Say not 'twas Agamemnon's wife
That so cut short his fated life,
It was the Alastor, whose dread mien
Took up the likeness of the queen.
Of that dark house 'twas he, 'twas he,
The curse and awful Destiny ;
(Where, father of that race unblest,
Old Atreus held his cannibal feast ;)
Wreaking for that dread crime the vengeance due,
The full-grown man for those poor babes he slew.

SEMICHORUS.

Who shall absolve thee from the guilt
Of that red blood so foully spilt ?
How, how the Alastor wouldst thou name,
Accomplice in that deed of shame ?
Ancient hereditary foe
Of all that house of guilt and woe ;
(Borne on the overwhelming flood,
Rushing amain, of kindred blood
Like clashing tides of meeting water,)
Burst Ares forth, black god of slaughter ;
On speeds he furious, o'er the rest,
Melting the congealed gore of the child-devouring feast.

CHORUS.

Alas ! alas ! how shall I mourn for thee ?
How my fond heart speak all its agony ?

There liest thou; thy cold corpse around
The subtle spider's web is wound;
Thy noble life thou didst outbreathe
By a most impious and unholy death.

SEMICHORUS.

Woe's me! woe's me! on that base bed
Unseemly for a kingly head,
Thou liest, by fraud to death trepanned
By that two-edged axe held in that murderous hand.

CLYTEMNESTRA.

It was not so; that man of pride!
By no unseemly death he died.
Who first into our household brought
Dark Ate's snares? who earliest taught
That fateful lesson of deceit,
   Decoying forth that child of many tears,
   Iphigenia, in her tender years?
Evil he did, evil is vengeance meet!
He will not make his insolent boast in Hell;
For with the sword he smote, and by the sword he fell.

SEMICHORUS.

In doubt, and dread, and grief I'm lost,
From care to care all helpless tost;
Where shall I turn? whence succour call?
The whole house tottering to its fall.

The showers of blood pour down amain
(Ceased hath the gentle dropping rain)—
Down, down with rattling noise it breaks,
The palace' deep foundation quakes:
Fate still her restless whetstone plies,
Whetting to sharper edge her sharpest agonies.

CHORUS.

Woe, woe! earth, earth! will thou not swallow me
Ere I am forced my kingly lord to see
Within that bath, with silver walled,
On his low bed unhonoured and unpalled?
 Oh, who will bury him?
 Oh, who will mourn for him?
Wilt thou, wilt thou, thou daring one, presume—
 Thou, thine own husband's bloody murderess!
To stand and wail as mourner by his tomb?
 With graceless grace, unholy holiness,
For noble funeral rites the unblest offerings bless.

SEMICHORUS.

Who o'er the godlike man shall raise
The lofty funeral chant of praise?
Mingled with bitter tears of ruth,
Utter from the full heart the noble truth?

CLYTEMNESTRA.

Speak not in this unseemly tone;
'Tis not thy care, 'tis ours alone.

By us he fell, by us he died ;
We the fit burial will provide ;
But not with tears or wailing din,
Without the palace and within.
Him shall Iphigenia greet ;
His daughter ! aye ! for thus 'tis meet ;
Down by the darksome fords below,
O'er the swift-flowing river of woe ;
And with her outspread arms embrace,
And fondly kiss her father's face.

CHORUS.

Taunt upon taunt ! mockery on mockery !
These clashing sayings are too hard for me !
The doer suffering still hath met,
Ever the murderer pays his debt.
'Tis the iron law enrolled above,
It is the fixed decree of Jove.
Though time may bide, Jove bides the time ;
Woe's done to him who doeth crime.
Who shall the old ancestral curse expel,
Within this house for ever doomed to dwell ?
Who shall release her from her bondage state,
Riveted for ever to her doleful fate ?

CHORUS.

Woe, woe ! earth, earth ! wilt thou not swallow me
Ere I am forced my kingly lord to see

Within that bath, with silver walled,
On his low bed unhonoured and unpalled?
    Oh, who will bury him?
    Oh, who will mourn for him?
Wilt thou, wilt thou, thou daring one, presume—
   Thou, thine own husband's bloody murderess—
To stand and wail as mourner by his tomb?
   With graceless grace, unholy holiness,
For noble funeral rites the unblest offerings bless?

SEMICHORUS.

   Who o'er the godlike man shall raise
   The lofty funeral chant of praise?
   Mingled with bitter tears of ruth,
   Utter from the full heart the noble truth?

CLYTEMNESTRA.

Now on this man the oracle
Hath all fulfilled its deathly spell.
But I with solemn oath do now
For ever covenant and vow
With the great Dæmon of the place,
Dæmon of the Pleisthenid race,
To be content with scanty share
(Unbearable though 'tis to bear).
But that great Dæmon, on his side,
From this our house departing wide,

    Some other fated race shall haste
    With murther foul and bloody deeds to waste.
    Of all the treasures of our hoarded gold,
    Some slender pittance I am content to hold,
    Driving far off the murtherous rage
That hath possessed this house from age to age.

ÆGISTHUS.

O light propitious of this day, that brings
High justice in her train. Now may we say
The Gods, the avengers of man's guilt, look down
From the far heavens upon the sins of earth;
Beholding how that man lies there, enwrapt
In the Furies' fine-woven robes (glad sight to us!),
Paying the penalty of his father's craft.
For Atreus, this land's king, and that man's father,
My father, his own brother (I speak plainly),
Thyestes, in a strife for supreme power,
Drove into exile from his house and home.
Thyestes, the long-suffering, back returned,
And sat a suppliant by his native hearth.
And safe he dwelt and happy; safety it seemed
And happiness, that, dying, with his blood
He did not redden his own native soil.
But impious Atreus, father of this man,
With eager-seeming love, that was not love,
An hospitable feast of sacrifice
Made for my father, feast of reconcilement.

But for the holy victim of that feast
He served up to him his own children's flesh.
The extremities, the fingers, and the feet,
Unseen of those that sat at the high board,
Lay covered up in a close dish apart.
No sign betrayed; my father took and ate,
Ignorant, that meal fatal to all his race.
But when he knew the abominable deed,
He shrieked, and vomiting up the unnatural food,
Fell to the ground. Then on all Pelops' sons
(The festal board by his spurning heel o'erthrown)
Uttered the deep intolerable curse,
"So perish all the race of Pleisthenes!"*
And in this man ye see that curse fulfilled,
Low weltering as he lies in his death-trance;
And me the artisan of that just deed.
For us, too, with our miserable father,
Thirteen poor innocent and helpless children,
Me yet an infant in my swaddling clothes,
Did he drive forth to endless banishment.
But me, grown up, great justice did bring back,
And long, close at his gates, I watched this man,
Weaving in silence all my dark designs.
Now, 'twere a glorious thing for me to die,
Seeing him caught in justice' iron toils.

---

* In this obscure, perhaps mutilated passage, I have introduced, as did Mr. Symmons, what seemed wanting to make the sense clear.

CHORUS.

Ægisthus!—I do hold it impious
To insult the dead. With hand premeditate
Thou say'st thou hast done this piteous deed—thou only.
I say thy guilty head will not escape
The curses of the indignant populace,
Their curses, and their killing showers of stones.

ÆGISTHUS.

Thou speak'st that labourest at the lowest oar;
They hold the sway who sit on the high deck.
Old as ye are, and hard as 'tis to teach
Meek lesson to such greybeards, ye must learn
To speak the words of truth and soberness.
Chains and the dungeon, fastings on prison fare,
Are excellent physicians for proud minds.
Ye that can see so much, see ye not this?
Kick not against the pricks! ye strive in vain.

CHORUS.

Woman! for him, thy husband, chief of men,
Returning glorious from the battle-field,
(Shamefully first defiled his genial bed:)
Hast thou devised this miserable fate?

ÆGISTHUS.

Ye'll rue these words; beginnings they will be
Of bitter sorrows! There's no music in them.

Not like the voice of Orpheus is your voice.
His sweet tones all things followed in their joy;
Ye with your howlings would wake up and goad
To madness even the gentlest. But we'll tame you,
And ye shall crouch submissive at our feet.

CHORUS.

And thou in Argos, shalt thou tyrant be,
Who having cunningly devised this deed,
With thine own coward arm darest not achieve it?

ÆGISTHUS.

It was the woman's part to deal in guile:
Had I appeared, suspected as his foe—
His ancient well-known foe—all had been lost.
Now all is won: and, master of his wealth,
I will essay to rule the subject city.
I the unruliest and most pampered steed
Will bridle, and make bear the heaviest yoke;
Or hunger, that with dungeon-darkness dwells,
Pale prison-mate, shall see him meek and mild.

CHORUS.

Dastard and base! The man with thine own hand
Thou darest not slay. A woman—foul disgrace
She of her country and her country's gods!
Murdered him. O Orestes, seest thou yet
The blessed light of day? When wilt thou come,

By favouring fortune hither timely led,
To be the slayer of this bloody two.

ÆGISTHUS.

Speak ye thus? and do ye thus?—speedily shall ye repent.

CHORUS.

Up, my fellow-soldiers, up!—Up, the strife is not far off!

ÆGISTHUS.

*   *   *   *

CHORUS.

Up! and every one be ready,—with his drawn sword in his hand.

ÆGISTHUS.

With my drawn sword in my right hand,—I will not refuse to die.

CHORUS.

We accept the challenge! Die, then!—Be the day's good fortune ours!

CLYTEMNESTRA.

Stay thee, stay, of men the dearest!—let us work no further ill.
We should reap a doleful harvest—mowing down these wretched men.

There hath been enough of misery—not another drop of blood.
Go, ye old men, go! retire ye—to your fate-appointed homes,
Ere ye do some deed of mischief,—and so suffer as ye do.
What is done is done for ever;—we must bear it as we may.
Let who will go labour further—'tis enough, enough for us,
Smitten by the awful Dæmon,—in his overwhelming wrath.
Hear, and hearken to my counsel, though 'tis but a woman speaks.

ÆGISTHUS.

But shall thus 'gainst me these greybeards—pluck their idle flowers of speech,
Thus pour out their insolent language,—tempting wantonly their fate,
Wandering thus from sober reason,—bearding thus their lord and king?

CHORUS.

'Tis not for the sons of Argos—on a wicked man to fawn.

ÆGISTHUS.

But hereafter my dread presence—ye shall feel and ye shall fear.

CHORUS.

Not if the great Gods Orestes—hasten hitherward to send.

ÆGISTHUS.

Well I know the hopes of exiles—vainly for their homes athirst.

CHORUS.

Do it, do it; get fat and wanton ;—Justice' holy robe defile.

ÆGISTHUS.

'Tis your hour. Ye of your folly—soon shall pay us the full meed.

CHORUS.

Strut thou in thy boastful carriage,—like a cock beside his mate.

CLYTEMNESTRA.

Care not for those idle howlings ;—you and I will take the rule,
And will wisely order all things—in this ancient kingly house.

THE BACCHANALS.

THE BACCHANALS.

It is remarkable that "The Bacchanals" is the only surviving tragedy connected with the worship and mystic history of the God at whose festivals the dramatic representations at Athens were celebrated, and out of songs in whose honour both the tragedy and comedy of the Greeks are said to have had their origin: the only other drama relating to Bacchus is the most irreverent comedy of Aristophanes. It is not less remarkable how few dramas there seem to have been connected with the worship of Dionysus. Among the four plays, indeed, ascribed to Thespis, one was on the subject of Pentheus; Welcker conjectured that another, the 'Ηίθεοι, was on that of Lycurgus of Thrace. I do not find in the exhaustive catalogue of Welcker any other clearly Dionysian tragedy amongst the works of the earliest dramatic poets; but there were two trilogies of Æschylus (each with its satiric drama); one on Pentheus, Σεμέλη ή 'Υδροφόροι, Βάκχαι, Πενθεύς; one on Lycurgus, 'Ηδωνοί, Βασσαρίδες, Νεανίσκοι (die Græchischen Tragödien, p. 30; comp. p. 50). Sophocles, however, seems to have abstained from these subjects, unless his 'Υδροφόροι was on the myth of Semele. The loss of these Æschylean tragedies is to be deplored more than that of any of the poet's works, except perhaps his "Niobe." What must they have been, with his lofty fearlessness of religious conception, his massy power and grandeur, and his lyric language unrivalled in its rude picturesqueness? We would willingly know, too, how such a subject could have been treated by the grave and reverent Sophocles.

The "Bacchæ" appears to have been the only Dionysian drama of Euripides, though some of the later writers—Chæremon, Iophon, and others—attempted the subject.

Some reasons occur at once for this curious fact in the history of the Grecian drama. The greater Gods were not themselves the leading personages in Greek tragedy. They appeared indeed, but not as the chief actors. They hovered, as it were, over the scene, or stood aloof till their time was come, and then stood forth as the administrators of eternal justice, as executioners of the decrees of destiny, to urge on or to avert some awful catastrophe. It was the old kingly houses of Argos and Mycenæ, of Thebes and Athens, which swept in their gorgeous palls over the scene; their kings held the high places in the drama—men with whom their fellowmen could fully sympathise, at whose crimes they might shudder, at whose sorrows they might weep. Of the demigods, Hercules alone (I except, of course, that mysterious half-divine being, Prometheus) appears in the Trachiniæ, and the Hercules Furens is the chief personage in the tragedy of that name. In the " Alcestis " Hercules is a God. Dionysus, in his own festivals (except with the wicked Aristophanes), appears hardly more frequently or more prominently than the other gods of Olympus.

The Greek tragedies, too, were, with few exceptions (as " The Persæ " and the " Taking of Miletus "), drawn from the old epic poems: from the Trojan cycle, including the " Cypria," the " Æthiopis," the lesser " Iliad," the " Nostoi," and others; from the Theban cycle, with the fate of the house of Œdipus; from the Argonautics, and the rest. But there does not seem to have been any old Epopee on the myths about Bacchus. The Dionysiaca were of later date—those which relate to his Indian conquests not earlier than Alexander.

Besides this peculiar interest as the only Dionysian play, I do not scruple to rank the " Bacchæ," on the whole, in the highest place among the tragedies of Euripides. There may be passages, indeed, of more surpassing beauty in the " Medea " and the " Hippolytus; " in the " Alcestis " and " Iphigenia " of greater tenderness. I never could agree with my friend Lord Macaulay in his contemptuous depreciation of Euripides (his characteristic sentence will be familiar to many). I am not blind to the defects of Euripides as compared with the proper ideal of Greek tragedy: his prosaic rationalising philosophy, his degradation of the Chorus from its lofty office as a personage in the drama to a singer of lyrics which have no connection with the fable; yet I think that I understand the phrase of Aristotle, whether rendered "the most pathetic," or, as I would read, "most impassioned," of the Greek dramatists; and I agree with Mr. Coleridge (*Table Talk*, ii. 107): "His choruses may be faulty as choruses, but how beautiful and affecting as odes or songs." Yet even Lord Macaulay acknowledged the transcendent excellence of the "Bacchæ."

It is well known that in the "Christus Patiens," ascribed to Gregory of Nazianzum, there was a strange plagiarism from this play. Some of the lines which belong to Agave were transferred to the lamentation of the Virgin Mother over her Son, our Saviour. It is almost more extraordinary that this passage is wanting in our copies of the "Bacchæ;" as if, to conceal his pious theft, the writer had mutilated the original. Indeed, according to Elmsley (preface to the "Bacchæ"), all our MSS. of this play are transcripts of one. I have been audacious enough to endeavour to make restitution to the Heathen; and from the hints furnished by the "Christus Patiens," and of course other images more suited to her tragic state as the murderess of her son, to supply the speech of Agave, of course distinguishing it by a different type.

DRAMATIS PERSONÆ.

DIONYSUS.
CHORUS OF BACCHANALS.
TIRESIAS.
CADMUS.
PENTHEUS.
ATTENDANT.
MESSENGER.
SECOND MESSENGER.
AGAVE.

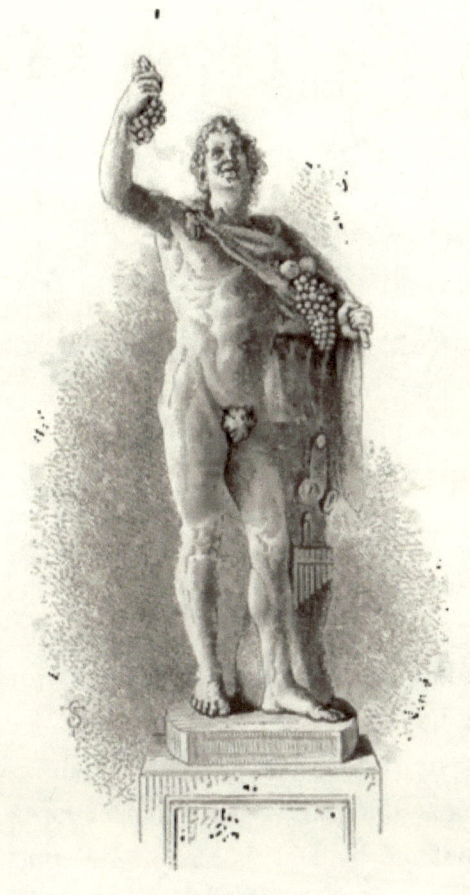

THE BACCHANALS.

DIONYSUS.

UNTO this land of Thebes I come, Jove's son,
Dionysus; he whom Semele of yore,
'Mid the dread midwifery of lightning fire,
Bore, Cadmus' daughter. In a mortal form,
The God put off, by Dirce's stream I stand,
And cool Ismenos' waters; and survey
My mother's grave, the thunder-slain, the ruins
Still smouldering of that old ancestral palace,
The flame still living of the lightning fire,
Here's immortal vengeance 'gainst my mother.
 And well hath reverent Cadmus set his ban
On that heaven-stricken, unapproached place,
His daughter's tomb, which I have mantled o'er
With the pale verdure of the trailing vine.
 And I have left the golden Lydian shores,

THE BACCHANALS.

The Phrygian and the Persian sun-seared plains,
And Bactria's walls; the Medes' wild wintery land
Have passed, and Araby the Blest; and all
Of Asia that along the salt sea-coast
Lifts up her high-towered cities, where the Greeks,
With the Barbarians mingled, dwell in peace.
   And everywhere my sacred choirs, mine Orgies
Have founded, by mankind confessed a God.
Now first in an Hellenic town I stand.
   Of all the Hellenic land here first in Thebes,
I have raised my revel shout, my fawn-skin donned,
Ta'en in my hand my thyrsus, ivy-crowned.
   But here, where least beseemed, my mother's sisters
Vowed Dionysus was no son of Jove;
That Semele, by mortal paramour won,
Belied great Jove as author of her sin;
'Twas but old Cadmus' craft: hence Jove in wrath
Struck dead the bold usurper of his bed.
   So from their homes I've goaded them in phrenzy;
Their wits all crazed, they wander o'er the mountains,
And I have forced them wear my wild attire.
There's not a woman of old Cadmus' race,
But I have maddened from her quiet house;
Unseemly mingled with the sons of Thebes,
On the roofless rocks, 'neath the pale pines, they sit.
   Needs must this proud recusant city learn,
In our dread Mysteries initiate,
Her guilt, and humbly seek to make atonement

To me, for Semele, mine outraged mother—
To me, the God confessed, of Jove begot.
   Old Cadmus now his might and kingly rule
To Pentheus hath given up, his sister's son,
My godhead's foe; who from the rich libation
Repels me, nor makes mention of my name
In holy prayer. Wherefore to him, to Thebes,
And all her sons, soon will I terribly show
That I am born a God: and so depart
(Here all things well disposed) to other lands,
Making dread revelation of myself.
   But if this Theban city, in her ire,
With arms shall seek to drive from off the mountains
My Bacchanal rout, at my wild Mænads' head
I'll meet, and mingle in the awful war.
Hence have I ta'en the likeness of a man,
Myself transmuted into human form.
   But ye, who Tmolus, Lydia's strength, have left
My Thyasus of women, whom I have led
From lands barbarian, mine associates here,
And fellow-pilgrims; lift ye up your drums,
Familiar in your native Phrygian cities,
Made by your mother Rhea's craft and mine;
And beat them all round Pentheus' royal palace,
Beat, till the city of Cadmus throngs to see.
I to the Bacchanals in the dim glens
Of wild Cithæron go to lead the dance.

CHORUS.

    From the Asian shore,
    And by the sacred steep of Tmolus hoar,
    Light I danced with wing-like feet,
    Toilless toil and labour sweet!
    Away! away! whoe'er he be ;
    Leave our path, our temple free !
    Seal up each silent lip in holy awe.
    But I, obedient to thy law,
O Dionysus! chant the choral hymn to thee.

    Blest above all of human line,
    Who, deep in mystic rites divine,
    Leads his hallowed life with us,
    Initiate in our Thyasus ;
    And, purified with holiest waters,
Goes dancing o'er the hills with Bacchus' daughters.
    And thy dark orgies hallows he,
    O mighty Mother, Cybele !
    He his thyrsus shaking round,
    All his locks with ivy crowned,
O Dionysus! boasts of thy dread train to be.

    Bacchanals! away, away!
    Lead your God in fleet array ;
    Bacchus lead, the ever young,
    A God himself from Gods that sprung,

From the Phrygian mountains down
Through every wide-squared Grecian town.

Him the Theban queen of yore
'Mid Jove's fast-flashing lightnings bore:
In her awful travail wild
Sprung from her womb the untimely child,
While smitten with the thunder-blast
The sad mother breathed her last.

Instant him Saturnian Jove
Received with all a mother's love;
In his secret thigh immured,
There with golden clasps secured,
Safe from Herè's jealous sight;
Then, as the Fates fulfilled, to light
He gave the horned god, and wound
The living snakes his brows around;

Whence still the wanded Mænads bear
Their serpent prey wreathed in their floating hair.

    Put on thy ivy crown,
    O Thebes, thou sacred town!
O hallowed house of dark-haired Semele!
    Bloom, blossom everywhere,
    With flowers and fruitage fair,
And let your phrenzied steps supported be
    With thyrsi from the oak
    Or the green ash-tree broke:
    Your spotted fawn-skins line with locks
    Torn from the snowy-fleeced flocks:
Shaking his wanton wand let each advance,
And all the land shall madden with the dance.

    Bromius, that his revel rout
    To the mountains leads about;
    To the mountains leads along,
    Where awaits the female throng;
    From the distaff, from the loom,
    Raging with the God they come.
    O ye mountains, wild and high,
    Where the old Kouretæ lie:
    Glens of Crete, where Jove was nurst,
    In your sunless caverns first
    The crested Korybantes found
    The leathern drums mysterious round,

That, mingling in harmonious strife
With the sweet-breathed Phrygian fife,
In Mother Rhea's hands they place,
Meet the Bacchic song to grace.
And the frantic Satyrs round
That ancient Goddess leap and bound:
And soon the Trieteric dances light
Began, immortal Bacchus' chief delight.

On the mountains wild 'tis sweet
When faint with rapid dance our feet;
Our limbs on earth all careless thrown
With the sacred fawn-skins strewn,
To quaff the goat's delicious blood,
A strange, a rich, a savage food.
Then off again the revel goes
O'er Phrygian, Lydian mountain brows;
Evoë! Evoë! leads the road,
Bacchus self the maddening God!

And flows with milk the plain, and flows with wine,
Flows with the wild bees' nectar-dews divine ;
And soars, like smoke, the Syrian incense pale—
　　The while the frantic Bacchanal

　　The beaconing pine-torch on her wand
　　Whirls around with rapid hand,
　　And drives the wandering dance about,
　　Beating time with joyous shout,
　　And casts upon the breezy air
　　All her rich luxuriant hair ;
　　Ever the burthen of her song,
　　" Raging, maddening, haste along
　　Bacchus' daughters, ye the pride
　　Of golden Tmolus' fabled side ;
　　While your heavy cymbals ring,
　　Still your "Evoë! Evoë!' sing!"
　　Evoë! the Evian god rejoices
　　In Phrygian tones and Phrygian voices,

When the soft holy pipe is breathing sweet,
    In notes harmonious to her feet,
Who to the mountain, to the mountain speeds;
Like some young colt that by its mother feeds,
    Gladsome with many a frisking bound,
The Bacchanal goes forth and treads the echoing ground.

TIRESIAS.

Ho! some one in the gates, call from his palace
Cadmus, Agenor's son, who, Sidon's walls
Leaving, built up this towered city of Thebes.
Ho! some one say, "Tiresias awaits him."
Well knows he why I am here; the covenant
Which I, th' old man, have made with him still older,
To lift the thyrsus wand, the fawn-skin wear,
And crown our grey hairs with the ivy-leaves.

CADMUS.

Best friend! with what delight within my palace
I heard thy speech, the speech of a wise man!
Lo! I am here, in the Gods' sacred garb;
For needs must we, the son of mine own daughter,
Dionysus, now 'mongst men a manifest God,
Even to the utmost of our power extol.
Where shall we lead the dance, plant the light foot,
And shake the hoary locks? Tiresias, thou
The aged lead the aged : wise art thou.
Nor will I weary night and day the earth

Beating with my lithe thyrsus. Oh, how sweetly!
Will we forget we are old!

TIRESIAS.

Thou'rt as myself:
I too grow young; I too essay the dance.

CADMUS.

Shall we, then, in our chariots seek the mountains?

TIRESIAS.

It were not the same homage to the God.

CADMUS.

The old man still shall be the old man's tutor.

TIRESIAS.

The God will guide us thither without toil.

CADMUS.

Of all the land, join we alone the dance?

TIRESIAS.

All else misjudge; we only are the wise.

CADMUS.

Too long we linger; hold thou fast mine hand.

TIRESIAS.

Lo! thus true yoke-fellows join hand with hand.

CADMUS.

I, mortal-born, may not despise the Gods.

TIRESIAS.

No wile, no paltering with the deities.
The ancestral faith, coeval with our race,
No subtle reasoning, if it soar aloft
Even to the height of wisdom, can o'erthrow.
Some one will say that I disgrace mine age,
Rapt in the dance, and ivy-crowned my head.
The Gods admit no difference: old or young,
All it behoves to mingle in the rite.
From all he will receive the common honour,
Nor deign to count his countless votaries.

CADMUS.

Since thou, Tiresias, seest not day's sweet light,
I, as thy Seer, must tell thee what is coming.
Lo, Pentheus, hurrying homewards to his palace,
Echion's son, to whom I have given the kingdom.
He is strangely moved! what new thing will he say?

PENTHEUS.

I have been absent from this land, and hear
Of strange and evil doings in the city.
Our women all have left their homes, to join
These fabled mysteries. On the shadowy rocks
Frequent they sit, this God of yesterday,
Dionysus, whosoe'er he be, with revels
Dishonourable honouring. In the midst
Stand the crowned goblets; and each stealing forth,
This way and that, creeps to a lawless bed;
In pretext, holy sacrificing Mænads,
But serving Aphrodite more than Bacchus.
All whom I've apprehended, in their gyves
Our officers guard in the public prison.
Those that have 'scaped I'll hunt from off the mountains,
Ino, Agave who to Echion bare me,
Her too, Autonoe, Antæus' mother;
And fettering them all in iron bonds,
I'll put an end to their mad wickedness.
'Tis said a stranger hath appeared among us,
A wizard, sorcerer, from the land of Lydia,
Beauteous with golden locks and purple cheeks,
Eyes moist with Aphrodite's melting fire.
And day and night he is with the throng, to guile
Young maidens to the soft inebriate rites.
    But if I catch him 'neath this roof, I'll silence
The beating of his thyrsus, stay his locks'

Wild tossing, from his body severing his neck.
He, say they, is the new God, Dionysus,
That was sewn up within the thigh of Jove.
He, with his mother, guiltily that boasted
Herself Jove's bride, was blasted by the lightning.
Are not such deeds deserving the base halter?
Sin heaped on sin! whoe'er this stranger be.

    But lo, new wonders! see I not Tiresias,
The prophet, in the dappled fawn-skin clad?
My mother's father too (a sight for laughter!),
Tossing his hair? My sire, I blush for thee,
Beholding thine old age thus fatuous grown.
Wilt not shake off that ivy? free thine hand
From that unseemly wand, my mother's father!
This is thy work, Tiresias. This new God
Wilt thou instal 'mongst men, at higher price
To vend new auspices, and well-paid offerings.
If thine old age were not thy safeguard, thou
Shouldst pine in chains among the Bacchanal women.
False teacher of new rites! For where 'mong women
The grape's sweet poison mingles with the feast,
Nought holy may we augur of such worship.

CHORUS.

Oh impious! dost thou not revere the Gods,
Nor Cadmus, who the earth-born harvest sowed?
Echion's son! how dost thou shame thy lineage!

TIRESIAS.

'Tis easy to be eloquent, for him
That's skilled in speech, and hath a stirring theme.
Thou hast the flowing tongue as of a wise man,
But there's no wisdom in thy fluent words;
For the bold demagogue, powerful in speech,
Is but a dangerous citizen, lacking sense.
This the new deity thou laugh'st to scorn,
I may not say how mighty he will be
Throughout all Hellas. Youth! there are two things
Man's primal need, Demeter, the boon Goddess,
(Or rather will ye call her Mother Earth?)
With solid food maintains the race of man.
He, on the other hand, the son of Semele,
Found out the grape's rich juice, and taught us mortals
That which beguiles the miserable of mankind
Of sorrow, when they quaff the vine's rich stream.
Sleep too, and drowsy oblivion of care
He gives, all-healing medicine of our woes.
He 'mong the Gods is worshipped a great God,
Author confessed to man of such rich blessings.
Him dost thou laugh to scorn, as in Jove's thigh
Sewn up, this truth profound will I unfold.
When Jove had snatched him from the lightning-fire,
He to Olympus bore the new-born babe.
Stern Heré strove to thrust him out of heaven,
But Jove encountered her with wiles divine:
He clove off part of th' earth-encircling air,

There Dionysus placed, the pleasing hostage,
Aloof from jealous Herè. So men said
Hereafter he was cradled in Jove's thigh
(From the assonance of words in our old tongue
For thigh and hostage the wild fable grew).*
A prophet is our God, for Bacchanalism
And madness are alike prophetical.
And when the God comes down in all his power,
He makes the mad to rave of things to come.
Of Ares he hath attributes: he the host
In all its firm array and serried arms,
With panic fear scatters, ere lance cross lance:
From Dionysus springs this frenzy too.

And him shall we behold on Delphi's crags
Leaping, with his pine-torches lighting up
The rifts of the twin-headed rock; and shouting
And shaking all around his Bacchic wand,
Great through all Hellas. Pentheus! be advised!
Vaunt not thy power o'er man, even if thou thinkest
That thou art wise (it is diseased, thy thought),
Think it not! In the land receive the God.
Pour wine, and join the dance, and crown thy brows.
Dionysus does not force our modest matrons
To the soft Cyprian rites; the chaste by nature
Are not so cheated of their chastity.
Think well of this, for in the Bacchic choir

---

* Ὅμηρος and ὁ μῆρος. This is a curious instance of the incipient rationalising spirit in Euripides, sadly misplaced in poetry.

The holy woman will not be less holy.
Thou'rt proud, when men to greet thee throng the gates,
And the glad city welcomes Pentheus' name,
He too, I ween, delights in being honoured.

   I, therefore, and old Cadmus whom thou mock'st,
Will crown our heads with ivy, dance along
An hoary pair—for dance perforce we must;
I war not with the Gods. Follow my counsel
Thou'rt at the height of madness, there's no medicine
Can minister to disease so deep as thine.

CHORUS.

Old man! thou sham'st not Phœbus thine own God.
Wise art thou worshipping that great God Bromius.

CADMUS.

My son! Tiresias well hath counselled thee;
Dwell safe with us within the pale of law.
Now thou fliest high: thy sense is void of sense.
Even if, as thou declar'st, he were no God,
Call thou him God. It were a splendid falsehood
If Semele be thought t' have borne a God;
'Twere honour unto us and to our race.
Hast thou not seen Actæon's wretched fate?
The dogs he bred, who fed from his own board,
Rent him in wrath to pieces; for he vaunted
Than Artemis to be a mightier hunter.

So do not thou : come, let me crown thine head
With ivy, and with us adore the god.

PENTHEUS.

Hold off thine hand ! away ! go rave and dance,
And wipe not off thy folly upon me.
On him, thy folly's teacher, I will wreak
Instant relentless justice. Some one go,
The seats from which he spies the flight of birds,
False augur, with the iron forks o'erthrow,
Scattering in wild confusion all abroad,
And cast his chaplets to the winds and storms ;
Thou'lt gall him thus, gall to the height of bitterness.
Ye to the city ! seek that stranger out,
That womanly man, who with this new disease
Afflicts our matrons, and defiles their beds :
Seize him, and bring him hither straight in chains,
That he may suffer stoning, that dread death.
Such be his woful Orgies here in Thebes.

TIRESIAS.

Oh, miserable ! that know'st not what thou sayest,
Crazed wert thou, now thou'rt at the height of
    madness :
But go we, Cadmus, and pour forth our prayer,
Even for this savage and ungodly man ;
And for our city, lest the God o'ertake us
With some strange vengeance.

Come with thy ivy staff,
Lean thou on me, and I will lean on thee :
'Twere sad for two old men to fall, yet go
We must, and serve great Bacchus, son of Jove.
What woe, O Cadmus, will this woe-named man*
Bring to thine house! I speak not now as prophet,
But a plain simple fact : fools still speak folly.

CHORUS.

Holy Goddess! Goddess old!
Holy! thou the crown of gold
In the nether realm that wearest,
Pentheus' awful speech thou hearest,
Hearest his insulting tone
'Gainst Semele's immortal son,
Bromius, of Gods the first and best.
At every gay and flower-crowned feast,
His the dance's jocund strife,
And the laughter with the fife,
Every care and grief to lull,
When the sparkling wine-cup full
Crowns the Gods' banquets, or lets fall
Sweet sleep on the eyes of men at mortal festival.

Of tongue unbridled without awe,
Of madness spurning holy law,

* A play upon the word Pentheus, from πένθος, sorrow.

Sorrow is the Jove-doomed close;
But the life of calm repose
And modest reverence holds her state
Unbroken by disturbing fate;
And knits whole houses in the tie
Of sweet domestic harmony.
Beyond the range of mortal eyes
'Tis not wisdom to be wise.
Life is brief, the present clasp,
Nor after some bright future grasp.
Such were the wisdom, as I ween
Only of frantic and ill-counselled men.

Oh, would to Cyprus I might roam,
　　Soft Aphrodite's isle,
Where the young Loves have their perennial
　　　home,
　That soothe men's hearts with tender guile:
Or to that wondrous shore where ever
The hundred-mouthed barbaric river,
Makes teem with wealth the showerless land!
O lead me! lead me, till I stand,
Bromius! sweet Bromius! where high swelling
Soars the Pierian Muses' dwelling—
Olympus' summit hoar and high—
Thou revel-loving Deity!
　　For there are all the Graces,
　　　And sweet Desire is there,

And to those hallowed places,
To lawful rites the Bacchanals repair.
The Deity, the son of Jove,
  The banquet is his joy,
Peace, the wealth-giver, doth he love,
  That nurse of many a noble boy.
Not the rich man's sole possessing;
To the poor the painless blessing
Gives he of the wine-cup bright.
Him he hates, who day and night,
Gentle night, and gladsome day,
Cares not thus to while away.
Be thou wisely unsevere!
Shun the stern and the austere!

Follow the multitude;
Their usage still pursue!
Their homely wisdom rude,
(Such is my sentence), is both right and true.

OFFICER.

Pentheus! we are here! In vain we went not forth;
The prey which thou commandest we have taken.
Gentle our quarry met us, nor turned back
His foot in flight, but held out both his hands;
Became not pale, changed not his ruddy colour.
Smiling he bade us bind, and lead him off,
Stood still, and made our work a work of ease.
Reverent I said, "Stranger, I arrest thee not
Of mine own will, but by the king's command."
But all the Bacchanals, whom thou hadst seized
And bound in chains within the public prison,
All now have disappeared, released they are leaping
In their wild Orgies, hymning the God Bacchus.
Spontaneous fell the chains from off their feet;
The bolts drew back untouched by mortal hand.
In truth this man, with many wonders rife
Comes to our Thebes. 'Tis thine t' ordain the rest.

PENTHEUS.

Bind fast his hands! Thus in his manacles
Sharp must he be indeed to 'scape us now.
There's beauty, stranger! woman-witching beauty

(Therefore thou art in Thebes) in thy soft form,
Thy fine bright hair, not coarse like the hard athlete's,
Is mantling o'er thy cheek warm with desire;
And carefully thou hast cherished thy white skin;
Not in the sun's swart beams, but in cool shade,
Wooing soft Aphrodite with thy loveliness.
But tell me first, from whence hath sprung thy race?

DIONYSUS.

There needs no boast; 'tis easy to tell this:
Of flowery Tmolus hast thou haply heard?

PENTHEUS.

Yea! that which girds around the Sardian city.

DIONYSUS.

Thence am I come, my country Lydia.

PENTHEUS.

Whence unto Hellas bringest thou thine Orgies?

DIONYSUS.

Dionysus, son of Jove, hath hallowed them.

PENTHEUS.

Is *there* a Jove then, that begets new Gods?

DIONYSUS.

No, it was *here* he wedded Semele.

PENTHEUS.

Hallowed he them by night, or in the eye of day?

DIONYSUS.

In open vision he revealed his Orgies.

PENTHEUS.

And what, then, is thine Orgies' solemn form?

DIONYSUS.

That is not uttered to the uninitiate.

PENTHEUS.

What profit, then, is theirs who worship him?

DIONYSUS.

Thou mayst not know, though precious were that knowledge.

PENTHEUS.

A cunning tale, to make me long to hear thee.

DIONYSUS.

The Orgies of our God scorn impious worshippers.

PENTHEUS.

Thou saw'st the manifest God! What was his form?

DIONYSUS.

Whate'er he would! it was not mine to choose.

PENTHEUS.

Cleverly blinked our question with no answer.

DIONYSUS.

Who wiseliest speaks, to the fool speaks foolishness.

PENTHEUS.

And hither com'st thou first with thy new God?

DIONYSUS.

There's no Barbarian but adores these rites.

PENTHEUS.

Being much less wise than we Hellenians.

DIONYSUS.

In this more wise. Their customs differ much.

PENTHEUS.

Performest thou these rites by night or day?

DIONYSUS.

Most part by night—night hath more solemn awe.

PENTHEUS.

A crafty rotten plot to catch our women.

DIONYSUS.

Even in the day bad men can do bad deeds.

PENTHEUS.

Thou of thy wiles shalt pay the penalty.

DIONYSUS.

Thou of thine ignorance—impious towards the Gods!

PENTHEUS.

He's bold, this Bacchus—ready enough in words.

DIONYSUS.

What penalty? what evil wilt thou do me?

PENTHEUS.

First will I clip away those soft bright locks.

DIONYSUS.

My locks are holy, dedicate to my God.

PENTHEUS.

Next, give thou me that thyrsus in thine hand.

DIONYSUS.

Take it thyself; 'tis Dionysus' wand.

PENTHEUS.

I'll bind thy body in strong iron chains.

DIONYSUS.

My God himself will loose them when he will.

PENTHEUS.

When thou invok'st him 'mid thy Bacchanals.

DIONYSUS.

Even now he is present; he beholds me now.

PENTHEUS.

Where is he then? mine eyes perceive him not.

DIONYSUS.

Near me: the impious eyes may not discern him.

PENTHEUS.

Seize on him, for he doth insult our Thebes.

DIONYSUS.

I warn thee, bind me not; the insane, the sane.

PENTHEUS.

I, stronger than thou art, say I will bind thee.

DIONYSUS.

Thou know'st not where thou art, or what thou art.

PENTHEUS.

Pentheus, Agave's son, my sire Echion.

DIONYSUS.

Thou hast a name whose very sound is woe.

PENTHEUS.

Away! go bind him in our royal stable,
That he may sit in midnight gloom profound:
There lead thy dance! But those thou hast hither led,
Thy guilt's accomplices, we'll sell for slaves;
Or, silencing their noise and beating drums,
As handmaids to the distaff, set them down.

DIONYSUS.

Away then! 'tis not well I bear such wrong;
The vengeance for this outrage he will wreak,
Whose being thou deniest, Dionysus:
Outraging me, ye bind him in your chains.

CHORUS.

Holy virgin-haunted water!
Ancient Achelous' daughter!
Dirce! in thy crystal wave
Thou the child of Jove didst lave.

Thou, when Zeus, his awful sire,
Snatched him from the immortal fire;
And locked him up within his thigh,
With a loud but gentle cry—
"Come, my Dithyrambus, come,
Enter thou the masculine womb!"
   Lo! to Thebes I thus proclaim,
"Twice born!" thus thy mystic name.

Blessed Dirce! dost thou well
From thy green marge to repel
Me, and all my jocund round,
With their ivy garlands crowned.
    Why dost fly me?
    Why deny me?
By all the joys of wine I swear,
Bromius still shall be my care.

Oh, what pride! pride unforgiven
Manifests, against high heaven
Th' earth-born, whom in mortal birth
'Gat Echion, son of earth;
Pentheus of the dragon brood,
Not of human flesh and blood;
But portent dire, like him whose pride,
The Titan, all the Gods defied.
Me, great Bromius' handmaid true;
Me, with all my festive crew,
Thralled in chains, he still would keep
In his palace dungeon deep.

Seest thou this, O son of Jove,
Dionysus, from above?
Thy rapt prophets dost thou see,
At strife with dark necessity?
    The golden wand
    In thy right hand.
Come, come thou down Olympus' side,
And quell the bloody tyrant in his pride.

Art thou holding revel now
On Nysas' wild-beast-haunted brow?
Is't thy Thyasus that clambers
O'er Corycia's mountain-chambers?
Or on Olympus, thick with wood,
With his harp where Orpheus stood,

And led the forest trees along,
Led the wild beasts with his song.
  O Pieria, blessed land,
Evius hallows thee, advancing,
With his wild choir's mystic dancing.
  Over rapid Axius' strand
He shall pass; o'er Lydia's tide
Then his whirling Mænads guide.
Lydia, parent boon of health,
Giver to man of boundless wealth;
Washing many a sunny mead,
Where the prancing coursers feed.

DIONYSUS.

What ho! what ho! ye Bacchanals!
Rouse and wake! your master calls.

CHORUS.

Who is here? and what is he
  That calls upon our wandering train?

DIONYSUS.

What ho! what ho! I call again!
The son of Jove and Semele.

CHORUS.

What ho! what ho! our Lord and Master:
Come, with footsteps fast and faster,

Join our revel! Bromius, speed,
Till quakes the earth beneath our tread.
  Alas! alas!
Soon shall Pentheus' palace wall,
Shake and crumble to its fall.

DIONYSUS.

Bacchus treads the palace floor!
Adore him!

CHORUS.

  Oh! we do adore!
 Behold! behold!
The pillars with their weight above,
Of ponderous marble, shake and move.
Hark! the trembling roof within
Bacchus shouts his mighty din.

DIONYSUS.

The kindling lamp of the dark lightning bring!
Fire, fire the palace of the guilty king.

CHORUS.

Behold! behold! it flames! do ye not see,
Around the sacred tomb of Semele,
 The blaze, that left the lightning there,
 When Jove's red thunder fired the air?
  On the earth, supine and low,
  Your shuddering limbs, ye Mænads, throw!

The king, the Jove-born god, destroying all,
In widest ruin strews the palace wall.

DIONYSUS.

O, ye Barbarian women, thus prostrate in dismay;
Upon the earth ye've fallen! See ye not, as ye may,
How Bacchus Pentheus' palace in wrath hath shaken down?
Rise up! rise up! take courage—shake off that trembling swoon.

CHORUS.

O light that goodliest shinest—over our mystic rite,
In state forlorn we saw thee—saw with what deep affright!

DIONYSUS.

How to despair ye yielded—as I boldly entered in
To Pentheus, as if captured, into the fatal gin.

CHORUS.

How could I less? who guards us—if thou shouldst come to woe?
But how wast thou delivered—from thy ungodly foe?

DIONYSUS.

Myself, myself delivered—with ease and effort slight.

CHORUS.

Thy hands, had he not bound them—in halters strong and tight?

DIONYSUS.

'Twas even then I mocked him ;—he thought me in his
   chain ;
He touched me not, nor reached me—his idle thoughts
   were vain !
In the stable stood a heifer—where he thought he had
   me bound ;
Round the beast's knees his cords—and cloven hoofs he
   wound.
Wrath-breathing, from his body—the sweat fell like a
   flood : .
He bit his lips in fury—while I beside who stood,
Looked on in unmoved quiet.
                           As at that instant come,
Shook Bacchus the strong palace ;—and on his mother's
   tomb
Flames kindled. When he saw it—on fire the palace
   deeming,
Hither he rushed, and thither—for " water, water"
   screaming.
And every slave 'gan labour—but laboured all in vain.
The toil he soon abandoned.—As though I had fled
   amain
He rushed into the palace—in his hand the dark sword
   gleamed ;
Then, as it seemed, great Bromius—I say ; but, as it
   seemed,

In the hall a bright light kindled—on that he rushed, and there,
As slaying me in vengeance—stood stabbing the thin air.
But then the avenging Bacchus—wrought new calamities;
From roof to base that palace—in smouldering ruin lies.
Bitter ruing our imprisonment—with toil forspent he threw
On earth his useless weapon.—Mortal, he had dared to do
'Gainst a God unholy battle.—But I in quiet state,
Unheeding Pentheus' anger—came through the palace gate.
It seems even now his sandal—is sounding on its way:
Soon is he here before us—and what now will he say?
With ease will I confront him—ire-breathing though he stand.
'Tis easy to a wise man—to practise self-command.

PENTHEUS.

I am outraged—mocked! The stranger hath escaped me,
Whom I so late had bound in iron chains.
Off, off! he is here! the man! how's this? how stands he
Before our palace, as just issuing forth?

DIONYSUS.

Stay thou thy step! Subdue thy wrath to peace!

PENTHEUS.

How, having burst thy chains, hast thou come forth?

DIONYSUS.

Said I not—heardst thou not? "There's one will free
  me!"

PENTHEUS.

What one? Thou speakest still words new and strange.

DIONYSUS.

He who for man plants the rich-tendrilled vine.

PENTHEUS.

Well layest thou this reproach on Dionysus.
Without there, close and bar the towers around.

DIONYSUS.

What! and the Gods! O'erleap they not all walls?

PENTHEUS.

Wise in all wisdom save in that thou shouldst have!

DIONYSUS.

In that I should have wisest still am I.
But listen first, and hear the words of him

Who comes to thee with tidings from the mountains.
Here will we stay   Fear not, we will not fly.

MESSENGER.

Pentheus, that rulest o'er this land of Thebes!
I come from high Cithæron, ever white
With the bright glittering snow's perennial rays.

PENTHEUS.

Why com'st thou? on what pressing mission bound?

MESSENGER.

I've seen the phrenzied Bacchanals, who had fled
On their white feet, forth goaded from the land.
I come to tell to thee and to this city
The awful deeds they do, surpassing wonder.
But answer first, if I shall freely say
All that's done there, or furl my prudent speech,
For thy quick temper I do fear, O king,
Thy sharp resentment and o'er-royal pride.

PENTHEUS.

Speak freely.   Thou shall part unharmed by me;
Wrath were not seemly 'gainst the unoffending.
But the more awful what thou say'st of these
Mad women, I the more on him, who hath guiled them
To their wild life, will wreak my just revenge.

MESSENGER.

Mine herds of heifers I was driving, slow
Winding their way along the mountain crags,
When the sun pours his full beams on the earth.
I saw three bands, three choirs of women: one
Autonoe led, thy mother led the second,
Agave—and the third Ino: and all
Quietly slept, their languid limbs stretched out:

Some resting on the ash-trees' stem their tresses;
Some with their heads upon the oak-leaves thrown
Careless, but not immodest; as thou sayest,
That drunken with the goblet and shrill fife
In the dusk woods they prowl for lawless love.
Thy mother, as she heard the horned steers
Deep lowing, stood up 'mid the Bacchanals
And shouted loud to wake them from their rest.
They from their lids shaking the freshening sleep,
Rose upright, wonderous in their decent guise,
The young, the old, the maiden yet unwed.

And first they loosed their locks over their shoulders,
Their fawn-skins fastened, wheresoe'er the clasps
Had lost their hold, and all the dappled furs
With serpents bound, that lolled out their lithe tongues.
Some in their arms held kid, or wild-wolf's cub,
Suckling it with her white milk; all the young mothers
Who had left their new-born babes, and stood with breasts
Full swelling: and they all put on their crowns
Of ivy, oak, or flowering eglantine.
One took a thyrsus wand, and struck the rock,
Leaped forth at once a dewy mist of water;
And one her rod plunged deep in the earth, and there
The God sent up a fountain of bright wine.
And all that longed for the white blameless draught
Light scraping with their finger-ends the soil
Had streams of exquisite milk; the ivy wands
Distilled from all their tops rich store of honey.
 Hadst thou been there, seeing these things, the God
Thou now revil'st, thou hadst adored with prayer.
 And we, herdsmen and shepherds, gathered around.
And there was strife among us in our words
Of these strange things they did, these marvellous things.
One city-bred, a glib and practised speaker,
Addressed us thus: "Ye that inhabit here
The holy mountain slopes, shall we not chase
Agave, Pentheus' mother, from the Bacchanals,
And win the royal favour?" Well to us
He seemed to speak; so, crouched in the thick bushes,

We lay in ambush. They at the appointed hour
Shook their wild thyrsi in the Bacchic dance,
"Iacchus" with one voice, the son of Jove,
"Bromius" invoking. The hills danced with them;
And the wild beasts; was nothing stood unmoved.
   And I leaped forth, as though to seize on her,
Leaving the sedge where I had hidden myself.
But she shrieked out, "Ho, my swift-footed dogs!
These men would hunt us down, but follow me—
Follow me, all your hands with thyrsi armed."
We fled amain, or by the Bacchanals
We had been torn in pieces. They with hands
Unarmed with iron, rushed on the browsing steers.
One ye might see a young and vigorous heifer
Hold, lowing in her grasp, like prize of war.
And some were tearing asunder the young calves;
And ye might see the ribs or cloven hoofs
Hurled wildly up and down, and mangled skins
Were hanging from the ash-boughs, dropping blood.
The wanton bulls, proud of their tossing horns
Of yore, fell stumbling, staggering to the ground,
Dragged down by the strong hands of thousand maidens.
And swifter were the entrails torn away
Than drop the lids over your royal eyeballs.
   Like birds that skim the earth, they glide along
O'er the wide plains, that by Asopus' streams
Shoot up for Thebes the rich and yellow corn;
And Hysiæ and Erythræ, that beneath

Cithæron's crag dwell lowly, like fierce foes
Invading, all with ravage waste and wide
Confounded; infants snatched from their sweet homes;
And what they threw across their shoulders, clung
Unfastened, nor fell down to the black ground.
No brass, nor ponderous iron: on their locks
Was fire that burned them not. Of those they spoiled
Some in their sudden fury rushed to arms.
Then was a mightier wonder seen, O king:
From them the pointed lances drew no blood.
But they their thyrsi hurling, javelin-like,
Drave all before, and smote their shameful backs,
Women drave men, but not without the God.

So did they straight return from whence they came,
Even to the fountains, which the God made flow;
Washed off the blood, and from their cheeks the drops
The serpents licked, and made them bright and clean.
This Godhead then, whoe'er he be, my master!
Receive within our city, great in all things.
In this I hear men say, he is the greatest,
He hath given the sorrow-soothing vine to man;
For where wine is not, love will never be,
Nor any other joy of human life.

CHORUS.

I am afraid to speak the words of freedom
Before the tyrant, yet it must be said,
" Inferior to no god is Dionysus."

PENTHEUS.

'Tis here then, like a wild fire, burning on,
This Bacchic insolence, Hellas' deep disgrace.
Off with delay!   Go to the Electrian gates
And summon all that bear the shield, and all
The cavalry upon their prancing steeds,
And those that couch the lance, and of the bow
Twang the sharp string.   Against these Bacchanals
We will go war.   It were indeed too much
From women to endure what we endure.

DIONYSUS.

Thou wilt not be persuaded by my words,
Pentheus! yet though of thee I have suffered wrong,
I warn thee, rise not up against the God.
Rest thou in peace.   Bromius will never brook
Ye drive his Mænads from their mountain haunts.

PENTHEUS.

Wilt teach me?   Better fly and save thyself,
Ere yet I wreak stern justice upon thee.

DIONYSUS.

Rather do sacrifice, than in thy wrath
Kick 'gainst the pricks—a mortal 'gainst a God.

PENTHEUS.

I'll sacrifice, and in Cithæron's glens,
As they deserve, a hecatomb of women.

DIONYSUS.

Soon will ye fly. 'Twere shame that shields of brass
Before the Bacchic thyrsi turn in rout.

PENTHEUS.

I am bewildered by this dubious stranger;
Doing or suffering, he holds not his peace.

DIONYSUS.

My friend! thou still mayest bring this to good end.

PENTHEUS.

How so? by being the slave of mine own slaves?

DIONYSUS.

These women—without force of arms, I'll bring them.

PENTHEUS.

Alas! he is plotting now some wile against me!

DIONYSUS.

But what if I could save thee by mine arts?

PENTHEUS.

Ye are all in league, that ye may hold your Orgies.

DIONYSUS.

I am in a league 'tis true, but with the God.

PENTHEUS.

Bring out mine armour! Thou! have done thy speech.

DIONYSUS.

Ha! wouldst thou see them seated on the mountains?

PENTHEUS.

Aye! for the sight give thousand weight of gold.

DIONYSUS.

Why hast thou fallen upon this strange desire?

PENTHEUS.

'Twere grief to see them in their drunkenness.

DIONYSUS.

Yet gladly wouldst thou see, what seen would grieve thee.

PENTHEUS.

Mark well! in silence seated neath the ash-trees.

DIONYSUS.

But if thou goest in secret they will scent thee.

PENTHEUS.

Best openly, in this thou hast said well.

DIONYSUS.

But if we lead thee, wilt thou dare the way?

PENTHEUS.

Lead on, and swiftly! let no time be lost!

DIONYSUS.

But first enwrap thee in these linen robes.

PENTHEUS.

What, will he of a man make me a woman?

DIONYSUS.

Lest they should kill thee, seeing thee as a man.

PENTHEUS.

Well dost thou speak; so spake the wise of old.

DIONYSUS.

Dionysus hath instructed me in this.

PENTHEUS.

How then can we best do what thou advisest?

DIONYSUS.

I'll enter in the house, and there array thee.

PENTHEUS.

What dress? a woman's? I am ashamed to wear it.

DIONYSUS.

Are thou not eager to behold the Mænads?

PENTHEUS.

And what dress say'st thou I must wrap around me?

DIONYSUS.

I'll smooth thine hair down lightly on thy brow.

PENTHEUS.

What is the second portion of my dress?

DIONYSUS.

Robes to thy feet, a bonnet on thine head.

PENTHEUS.

Wilt thou array me then in more than this?

DIONYSUS.

A thyrsus in thy hand, a dappled fawn-skin.

PENTHEUS.

I cannot clothe me in a woman's dress.

DIONYSUS.

Thou wilt have bloodshed, warring on the Mænads.

PENTHEUS.

'Tis right, I must go first survey the field.

DIONYSUS.

'Twere wiser than to hunt evil with evil.

PENTHEUS.

How pass the city, unseen of the Thebans?

DIONYSUS.

We'll go by lone byways; I'll lead thee safe.

PENTHEUS.

Aught better than be mocked by these loose Bacchanals.
When we come back, we'll counsel what were best.

DIONYSUS.

Even as you will: I am here at your command.

PENTHEUS.

So let us on; I must go forth in arms,
Or follow the advice thou givest me.

DIONYSUS.

Women! this man is in our net; he goes
To find his just doom 'mid the Bacchanals.
Dionysus! to thy work! thou'rt not far off;
Vengeance is ours. Bereave him first of sense;
Yet be his phrenzy slight. In his right mind
He never had put on a woman's dress;
But now, thus shaken in his mind, he'll wear it.
A laughing-stock I'll make him to all Thebes,
Led in a woman's dress through the wide city,
For those fierce threats in which he was so great.
But I must go, and Pentheus—in the garb
Which wearing, even by his own mother's hand
Slain, he goes down to Hades. Know he must
Dionysus, son of Jove, among the Gods
Mightiest, yet mildest to the sons of men.

CHORUS.

O when, through the long night,
With fleet foot glancing white,
Shall I go dancing in my revelry,
My neck cast back, and bare
Unto the dewy air,

Like sportive fawn in the green meadow's glee?
    Lo, in her fear she springs
    Over th' encircling rings,
Over the well-woven nets far off and fast;
    While swift along her track
    The huntsman cheers his pack,
With panting toil, and fiery storm-wind haste.
Where down the river-bank spreads the wide meadow,
    Rejoices she in the untrod solitude.
Couches at length beneath the silent shadow
    Of the old hospitable wood.

    What is wisest? what is fairest,
    Of God's boons to man the rarest?
    With the conscious conquering hand
    Above the foeman's head to stand.
    What is fairest still is dearest.

    Slow come, but come at length,
    In their majestic strength,
Faithful and true, the avenging deities:
    And chastening human folly,
    And the mad pride unholy,
Of those who to the Gods bow not their knees.
    For hidden still and mute,
    As glides their printless foot,
The impious on their winding path they hound.

For it is ill to know,
And it is ill to do,
Beyond the law's inexorable bound.
'Tis but light cost in his own power sublime
   To array the Godhead, whosoe'er he be ;
And Law is old, even as the oldest time,
   Nature's own unrepealed decree.

What is wisest ? what is fairest,
Of God's boons to man the rarest?
With the conscious conquering hand
Above the foeman's head to stand.
What is fairest still is rarest.

Who hath 'scaped the turbulent sea,
And reached the haven, happy he !
Happy he whose toils are o'er,
In the race of wealth and power!
This one here, and that one there,
Passes by, and everywhere
Still expectant thousands over
Thousand hopes are seen to hover.
Some to mortals end in bliss ;
   Some have already fled away :
Happiness alone is his,
   That happy is to-day.

DIONYSUS.

Thou art mad to see that which thou shouldst not see,
And covetous of that thou shouldst not covet.
Pentheus! I say, come forth! appear before me,
Clothed in the Bacchic Mænads' womanly dress;
Spy on thy mother and her holy crew,
Come like in form to one of Cadmus' daughters.

PENTHEUS.

Ha! now indeed two suns I seem to see,
A double Thebes, two seven-gated cities;
Thou, as a bull, seemest to go before me,
And horns have grown upon thine head. Art thou
A beast indeed? Thou seem'st a very bull.

DIONYSUS.

The God is with us; unpropitious once,
But now at truce: now seest thou what thou shouldst
 see?

PENTHEUS.

What see I? Is not that the step of Ino?
And is it not Agave there, my mother?

DIONYSUS.

Methinks 'tis even they whom thou behold'st;
But, lo! this tress hath strayed out of its place,
Not as I braided it, beneath thy bonnet.

PENTHEUS.

Tossing it this way now, now tossing that,
In Bacchic glee, I have shaken it from its place.

DIONYSUS.

But we, whose charge it is to watch o'er thee,
Will braid it up again. Lift up thy head.

PENTHEUS.

Braid as thou wilt, we yield ourselves to thee.

DIONYSUS.

Thy zone is loosened, and thy robe's long folds
Droop outward, nor conceal thine ankles now.

PENTHEUS.

Around my right foot so it seems, yet sure
Around the other it sits close and well.

DIONYSUS.

Wilt thou not hold me for thy best of friends,
Thus strangely seeing the coy Bacchanals?

PENTHEUS.

The thyrsus—in my right hand shall I hold it?
Or thus am I more like a Bacchanal?

DIONYSUS.

In thy right hand, and with thy right foot raise it.
I praise the change of mind now come o'er thee.

PENTHEUS.

Could I not now bear up upon my shoulders
Cithæron's crag, with all the Bacchanals?

DIONYSUS.

Thou couldst if 'twere thy will. In thy right mind
Erewhile thou wast not; now thou art as thou shouldst
    be.

PENTHEUS.

Shall I take levers, pluck it up with my hands,
Or thrust mine arm or shoulder 'neath its base?

DIONYSUS.

Destroy thou not the dwellings of the Nymphs,
The seats where Pan sits piping in his joy.

PENTHEUS.

Well hast thou said; by force we conquer not
These women. I'll go hide in yonder ash.

DIONYSUS.

Within a fatal ambush wilt thou hide thee,
Stealing, a treacherous spy, upon the Mænads.

PENTHEUS.

And now I seem to see them there like birds
Couching on their soft beds amid the fern.

DIONYSUS.

Art thou not therefore set as watchman o'er them?
Thou'lt seize them—if they do not seize thee first.

PENTHEUS.

Lead me triumphant through the land of Thebes!
I, only I, have dared a deed like this.

DIONYSUS.

Thou art the city's champion, thou alone.
Therefore a strife thou wot'st not of awaits thee.
Follow me! thy preserver goes before thee;
Another takes thee hence.

PENTHEUS.

   Mean'st thou my mother?

DIONYSUS.

Aloft shalt thou be borne.

PENTHEUS.

   O the soft carriage!

DIONYSUS.

In thy mother's hands.

PENTHEUS.

    Wilt make me thus luxurious?

DIONYSUS.

Strange luxury, indeed!

PENTHEUS.

    'Tis my desert.

DIONYSUS.

Thou art awful! awful! doomed to awful end!
Thy glory shall soar up to the high heavens!
    Stretch forth thine hand, Agave! ye her kin,
Daughters of Cadmus! to a terrible grave
Lead I this youth! myself shall win the prize—
Bromius and I; the event will show the rest.

CHORUS.

Ho! fleet dogs and furious to the mountains, ho!
Where their mystic revels Cadmus' daughters keep.
    Rouse them, goad them out,
'Gainst him, in woman's mimic garb concealed,
Gazer on the Mænads in their dark rites unrevealed.
First his mother shall behold him on his watch below,
From the tall tree's trunk or from the wild scaur steep;
    Fiercely will she shout—
" Who the spy upon the Mænads on the rocks that roam
To the mountain, to the mountain, Bacchanals, has come?"

Who hath borne him?
He is not of woman's blood,
The lioness?
Or the Lybian Gorgon's brood?
Come, Vengeance, come, display thee?
With thy bright sword array thee!
The bloody sentence wreak
On the dissevered neck
Of him who God, law, justice, hath not known,
Echion's earth-born son.

He, with thought unrighteous and unholy pride,
'Gainst Bacchus and his mother, their Orgies' mystic mirth
Still holds his frantic strife,
And sets him up against the God, deeming it light
To vanquish the invincible of might.
Hold thou fast the pious mind; so, only so, shall glide
In peace with Gods above, in peace with men on earth,
Thy smooth painless life.
I admire not, envy not, who would be overwise:
Mine be still the glory, mine be still the prize,
By night and day
To live of the immortal Gods in awe;
Who fears them not
Is but the outcast of all law.

Come, Vengeance, come display thee!
With thy bright sword array thee!

THE BACCHANALS. 157

    The bloody sentence wreak,
      On the dissevered neck
Of him who god, law, justice has not known,
    Echion's earth-born son.

    Appear! appear!
    Or as the stately steer!
    Or many-headed dragon be!
Or the fire-breathing lion, terrible to see.
Come, Bacchus, come 'gainst the hunter of the Bacchanals,
    Even now, now as he falls
Upon the Mænads' fatal herd beneath.
    With smiling brow,
    Around him throw
The inexorable net of death.

MESSENGER.

O house most prosperous once throughout all Hellas!
House of the old Sidonian! in this land*
Who sowed the dragon's serpent's earth-born harvest,
How I deplore thee! I a slave, for still
Grieve for their master's sorrows faithful slaves.

CHORUS.

What's this? aught new about the Bacchanals?

---

* The scene here manifestly changes back to Thebes.

MESSENGER.

Pentheus hath perished, old Echion's son.

CHORUS.

King Bromius, thou art indeed a mighty God!

MESSENGER.

What say'st thou? how is this? rejoicest thou
O woman! in my master's awful fate?

CHORUS.

Light chants the stranger her barbarous strains;
I cower not in fear for the menace of chains.

MESSENGER.

All Thebes thus void of courage deemest thou?

CHORUS.

O Dionysus! Dionysus! Thebes
Hath o'er me now no power.

MESSENGER.

'Tis pardonable, yet it is not well,
Woman! in others' miseries to rejoice.

CHORUS.

Tell me, then, by what fate died the unjust—
The man, the dark contriver of injustice?

MESSENGER.

Therapnæ having left the Theban city,
And passed along Asopus' winding shore,
We 'gan to climb Cithæron's upward steep—
Pentheus and I (I waited on my lord),
And he that led us on our quest, the stranger.
And first we crept along a grassy glade,
With silent footsteps, and with silent tongues,
Slow moving, as to see, not being seen.
There was a rock-walled glen, watered by a streamlet,
And shadowed o'er with pines; the Mænads there
Sate, all their hands busy with pleasant toil.
And some the leafy thyrsus, that its ivy
Had dropped away, were garlanding anew;
Like fillies some, unharnessed from the yoke;
Chanted alternate all the Bacchic hymn.
Ill-fated Pentheus, as he scarce could see
That womanly troop, spake thus: "Where we stand, stranger,
We see not well the unseemly Mænad dance:
But, mounting on a bank, or a tall tree,
Clearly shall I behold their deeds of shame."

A wonder then I saw that stranger do.
He seized an ash-tree's high heaven-reaching stem,
And dragged it down, dragged, dragged to the low earth;
And like a bow it bent. As a curved wheel
Becomes a circle in the turner's lathe,

The stranger thus that mountain tree bent down
To the earth, a deed of more than mortal strength.
Then seating Pentheus on those ash-tree boughs,
Upward he let it rise, steadily, gently
Through his hands, careful lest it shake him off;
And slowly rose it, upright to its height,
Bearing my master seated on its ridge.
There was he seen, rather than saw the Mænads,
More visible he could not be, seated aloft.
The stranger from our view had vanished quite.
Then from the heavens a voice, as it should seem
Dionysus, shouted loud, "Behold! I bring,
O maidens, him that you and me, our rites,
Our Orgies laughed to scorn; now take your vengeance."
And as he spake, a light of holy fire
Stood up, and blazed from earth straight up to heaven.
Silent the air, silent the verdant grove
Held its still leaves: no sound of living thing.
They, as their ears just caught the half-heard voice,
Stood up erect, and rolled their wondering eyes.
Again he shouted. But when Cadmus' daughters
Heard manifest the God's awakening voice,
Forth rushed they, fleeter than the winged dove,
Their nimble feet quick coursing up and down.
Agave first, his mother, then her kin,
The Mænads, down the torrent's bed, in the grove,
From crag to crag they leaped, mad with the God.
And first with heavy stones they hurled at him,

Climbing a rock in front; the branches some
Of the ash-tree darted; some like javelins
Sent their sharp thyrsi through the sounding air,
Pentheus their mark: but yet they struck him not;
His height still baffled all their eager wrath.
There sat the wretch, helpless in his despair.
The oaken boughs, by lightning as struck off,
Roots torn from the earth but with no iron wedge,
They hurled, but their wild labours all were vain.
Agave spake, "Come all, and stand around,
And grasp the tree, ye Mænads, soon we will seize
The beast that rides thereon. He will ne'er betray
The mysteries of our God." A thousand hands
Were on the ash, and tore it from the earth:
And he that sat aloft, down, headlong, down
Fell to the ground, with thousand piteous shrieks,
Pentheus, for well he knew his end was near.
His mother first began the sacrifice,
And fell on him. His bonnet from his hair
He threw, that she might know and so not slay him,
The sad Agave. And he said, her cheek
Fondling, "I am thy child, thine own, my mother!
Pentheus, whom in Echion's house you bare.
Have mercy on me, mother! for his sins,
Whatever be his sins, kill not thy son."
She, foaming at the mouth, her rolling eyeballs
Whirling around, in her unreasoning reason,
By Bacchus all possessed, knew, heeded not.

M

She caught him in her arms, seized his right hand,
And with her feet set on his shrinking side,
Tore out the shoulder, not with her own strength:
The God made easy that too cruel deed.
And Ino laboured on the other side,

Rending the flesh: Autonoe, all the rest,
Pressed fiercely on, and there was one wild din.
He groaning deep, while he had breath to groan,
They shouting triumph; and one bore an arm,
One a still-sandalled foot; and both his sides
Lay open, rent. Each in her bloody hand
Tossed wildly to and fro lost Pentheus' limbs.
The trunk lay far aloof, 'neath the rough rocks
Part, part amid the forest's thick-strewn leaves,
Not easy to be found. The wretched head,
Which the mad mother, seizing in her hands,
Had on a thyrsus fixed, she bore aloft

All o'er Cithæron, as a mountain lion's,
Leading her sisters in their Mænad dance.
And she comes vaunting her ill-fated chase
Unto these walls, invoking Bacchus still,
Her fellow-hunter, partner in her prey,
Her triumph—triumph soon to end in tears!
I fled the sight of that dark tragedy,
Hastening, ere yet Agave reached the palace.
Oh! to be reverent, to adore the Gods,
This is the noblest, wisest course of man,
Taking dread warning from this dire event.

CHORUS.

Dance and sing
In Bacchic ring,
Shout, shout the fate, the fate of gloom,
Of Pentheus, from the dragon born;
He the woman's garb hath worn,
Following the bull, the harbinger, that led him to his doom.
O ye Theban Bacchanals!
Attune ye now the hymn victorious,
The hymn all glorious,
To the tear, and to the groan!
O game of glory!
To bathe the hands besprent and gory,
In the blood of her own son.

But I behold Agave, Pentheus' mother,
Nearing the palace with distorted eyes.
Hail we the ovation of the Evian god.

AGAVE.

O ye Asian Bacchanals!

CHORUS.

Who is she on us who calls?

AGAVE.

From the mountains, lo! we bear
    To the palace gate
Our new-slain quarry fair.

CHORUS.

I see, I see, and on thy joy I wait.

AGAVE.

Without a net, without a snare,
The lion's cub, I took him there.

CHORUS.

In the wilderness, or where?

AGAVE.

Cithæron . . .

CHORUS.

Of Cithæron what?

AGAVE.

Gave him to slaughter.

CHORUS.

O blest Agave!

AGAVE.

In thy song extol me.

CHORUS.

Who struck him first?

AGAVE.

Mine, mine, the glorious lot.

CHORUS.

Who else?

AGAVE.

Of Cadmus

CHORUS.

What of Cadmus' **daughter?**

AGAVE.

With me, with me, did all the race
Hound the prey.

CHORUS.

O fortunate chase!

AGAVE.

The banquet share with me!

CHORUS.

Alas! what shall our banquet be?

AGAVE.

How delicate the kid and young!
The thin locks have but newly sprung
    Over his forehead fair.

CHORUS.

'Tis beauteous as the tame beasts' cherished hair.

AGAVE.

Bacchus, hunter known to fame!
    Did he not our Mænads bring
On the track of this proud game?
    A mighty hunter is our king!
Praise me! praise me!

CHORUS.

Praise I not thee?

AGAVE.

Soon with the Thebans all, the hymn of praise
  Pentheus my son will to his mother raise :
    For she the lion prey hath won,
    A noble deed and nobly done.

CHORUS.

  Dost thou rejoice ?

AGAVE.

    Aye with exulting voice
  My great, great deed I elevate,
    Glorious as great.

CHORUS.

Sad woman, to the citizens of Thebes
Now show the conquered prey thou bearest hither.

AGAVE.

Ye that within the high-towered Theban city
Dwell, come and gaze ye all upon our prey,
The mighty beast by Cadmus' daughter ta'en ;
Nor with Thessalian sharp-pointed javelins,
Nor nets, but with the white and delicate palms
Of our own hands. Go ye, and make your boast,
Trusting to the spear-maker's useless craft :
We with these hands have ta'en our prey, and rent
The mangled limbs of this grim beast asunder.

Where is mine aged sire? let him draw near!
And where is my son Pentheus? let him mount
On the broad stairs that rise before our house;
And on the triglyph nail this lion's head,
That I have brought him from our splendid chase.

CADMUS.

Follow me, follow, bearing your sad burthen,
My servants! Pentheus' body, to our house;
The body that with long and weary search
I found at length in lone Cithæron's glens;
Thus torn, not lying in one place, but wide
Scattered amid the dark and tangled thicket.
Already, as I entered in the city
With old Tiresias, from the Bacchanals,
I heard the fearful doings of my daughter.
And back returning to the mountain, bear
My son, thus by the furious Mænads slain.
Her who Actæon bore to Aristæus,
Autonoe, I saw, and Ino with her
Still in the thicket goaded with wild madness.
And some one said that on her dancing feet
Agave had come hither—true he spoke;
I see her now: O most unblessed sight!

AGAVE.

Father, 'tis thy peculiar peerless boast
Of womanhood the noblest t' have begot—

Me—me the noblest of that noble kin.
For I the shuttle and the distaff left
For mightier deeds—wild beasts with mine own hands
To capture. Lo! I bear within mine arms,
These glorious trophies, to be hung on high
Upon thy house : receive them, O my father!
Call thy friends to the banquet feast! Blest thou!
Most blest, through us who have wrought such splendid
 deeds.

CADMUS.

Measureless grief! eye may not gaze on it,
The slaughter wrought by those most wretched hands.
Oh! what a sacrifice before the Gods!
All Thebes, and us, thou callest to the feast.
Justly—too justly, hath king Bromius
Destroyed us, fatal kindred to our house.

AGAVE.

Oh! how morose is man in his old age,
And sullen in his mien. Oh! were my son
More like his mother, mighty in his hunting;
When he goes forth among the youth of Thebes
Wild beasts to chase! But he is great alone,
In warring on the Gods. We two, my sire,
Must counsel him against his evil wisdom.
Where is he? Who will call him here before us
That he may see me in my happiness?

CADMUS.

Woe! woe! when ye have sense of what ye have done,
With what deep sorrow, sorrow ye! To th' end
Oh! could ye be, only as now ye are,
Nor happy were ye deemed, nor miserable.

AGAVE.

What is not well? for sorrow what the cause?

CADMUS.

First lift thine eyes up to the air around.

AGAVE.

Behold! why thus commandest me to gaze?

CADMUS.

Is all the same? appears there not a change?

AGAVE.

'Tis brighter, more translucent than before.

CADMUS.

Is there the same elation in thy soul?

AGAVE.

I know not what thou mean'st; but I become
Conscious, my changing mind is settling down.

CADMUS.

Canst thou attend, and plainly answer me?

AGAVE.

I have forgotten, father, all I said.

CADMUS.

Unto whose bed wert thou in wedlock given?

AGAVE.

Echion's, him they call the Dragon-born.

CADMUS.

Who was the son to thy husband thou didst bear?

AGAVE.

Pentheus, in commerce 'twixt his sire and me.

CADMUS.

And whose the head thou holdest in thy hands?

AGAVE.

A lion's; thus my fellow-hunters said.

CADMUS.

Look at it straight: to look on't is no toil.

AGAVE.

What see I? Ha! what's this within my hands?

CADMUS.

Look on't again, again: thou wilt know too well.

AGAVE.

I see the direst woe that eye may see.

CADMUS.

The semblance of a lion bears it now?

AGAVE.

No: wretch, wretch that I am; 'tis Pentheus' head!

CADMUS.

Even ere yet recognised thou mightst have mourned him.

AGAVE.

Who murdered him? How came he in my hands?

CADMUS.

Sad truth! untimely dost thou ever come!

AGAVE.

Speak; for my heart leaps with a boding throb.

CADMUS.

'Twas thou didst slay him, thou and thine own sisters.

AGAVE.

Where died he? in his palace? in what place?

CADMUS.

There where the dogs Actæon tore in pieces.

AGAVE.

Why to Cithæron went the ill-fated man?

CADMUS.

To mock the God, to mock the Orgies there.

AGAVE.

But how and wherefore had we thither gone?

CADMUS.

In madness! the whole city maddened with thee.

AGAVE.

Dionysus hath destroyed us! late I learn it.

CADMUS.

Mocked with dread mockery; no God ye held him.

AGAVE.

Father! where's the dear body of my son?

CADMUS.

I bear it here, not found without much toil.

AGAVE.

Are all the limbs together, sound and whole?
And Pentheus, shared he in my desperate fury?

CADMUS.

Like thee he was, he worshipped not the God.
All, therefore, are enwrapt in one dread doom.
You, he, in whom hath perished all our house,
And I who, childless of male offspring, see
This single fruit—O miserable!—of thy womb
Thus shamefully, thus lamentably dead—
Thy son, to whom our house looked up, the stay
Of all our palace he, my daughter's son,
The awe of the whole city. None would dare
Insult the old man when thy fearful face
He saw, well knowing he would pay the penalty.
Unhonoured now, I am driven from out mine home;
Cadmus the great, who all the race of Thebes
Sowed in the earth, and reaped that harvest fair.
O best beloved of men, thou art now no more,
Yet still art dearest of my children thou!

No more, this grey beard fondling with thine hand,
Wilt call me thine own grandsire, thou sweet child,
And fold me round and say, " Who doth not honour
    thee?
Old man, who troubles or afflicts thine heart?
Tell me, that I may 'venge thy wrong, my father!"
Now wretchedest of men am I.   Thou pitiable—
More pitiable thy mother—sad thy kin.
O if there be who scorneth the great Gods,
Gaze on this death, and know that there are Gods.

CHORUS.

Cadmus, I grieve for thee.   Thy daughter's son
Hath his just doom—just, but most piteous.

AGAVE.

Father, thou seest how all is changed with me:
I am no more the Mænad dancing blithe,
I am but the feeble, fond, and desolate mother.
I know, I see—ah, knowledge best unknown!
Sight best unseen!—I see, I know my son,
Mine only son! alas! no more my son.
O beauteous limbs, that in my womb I bare!
O head, that on my lap wast wont to sleep!
O lips, that from my bosom's swelling fount
Drained the delicious and soft-oozing milk!
O hands, whose first use was to fondle me!
O feet, that were so light to run to me!

O gracious form, that men wondering beheld!
O haughty brow, before which Thebes bowed down!
O majesty! O strength! by mine own hands—
By mine own murderous, sacrilegious hands—
Torn, rent asunder, scattered, cast abroad!
O thou hard God! was there no other way
To visit us? Oh! if the son must die,
Must it be by the hand of his own mother?
If the impious mother must atone her sin,
Must it be but by murdering her own son?

DIONYSUS.

Now hear ye all, Thebes' founders, what is woven
By the dread shuttle of the unerring Fates.
Thou, Cadmus, father of this earth-born race,
A dragon shalt become; thy wife shall take
A brutish form, and sink into a serpent,
Harmonia, Ares' daughter, whom thou wedd'st,
Though mortal, as Jove's oracle declares.
Thou in a car by heifers drawn shalt ride,
And with thy wife, at the Barbarians' head:
And many cities with their countless host
Shall they destroy, but when they dare destroy
The shrine of Loxias, back shall they return
In shameful flight: but Ares guards Harmonia
And thee, and bears you to the Isles of the Blest.
  This say I, of no mortal father born,
Dionysus, son of Jove. Had ye but known

To have been pious when ye might, Jove's son
Had been your friend; ye had been happy still.

AGAVE.

Dionysus, we implore thee! we have sinned!

DIONYSUS.

Too late ye say so; when ye should, ye would not.

AGAVE.

That know we now; but thou'rt extreme in vengeance.

DIONYSUS.

Was I not outraged, being a God, by you?

AGAVE.

The Gods should not be like to men in wrath.

DIONYSUS.

This Jove, my father, long hath granted me.

AGAVE.

Alas, old man! our exile is decreed.

DIONYSUS.

Why then delay ye the inevitable?

CADMUS.

O child, to what a depth of woe we have fallen!
Most wretched thou, and all thy kin beloved!
I too to the Barbarians must depart
An aged denizen. For there's a prophecy,
'Gainst Hellas a Barbaric mingled host
Harmonia leads, my wife, daughter of Ares.
A dragon I, with dragon nature fierce,
Shall lead the stranger spearmen 'gainst the altars
And tombs of Hellas, nor shall cease my woes,
Sad wretch! not even when I have ferried o'er
Dark Acheron, shall I repose in peace.

AGAVE.

Father! to exile go I without thee?

CADMUS.

Why dost thou clasp me in thine arms, sad child,
A drone among the bees, a swan worn out?

AGAVE.

Where shall I go, an exile from my country?

CADMUS.

I know not, child; thy sire is a feeble aid.

AGAVE.

Farewell, mine home! Farewell, my native Thebes!
My bridal chamber! Banished, I go forth.

CADMUS.

To the house of Aristæus go, my child.

AGAVE.

I wait for thee, my father!

CADMUS.

                                I for thee!
And for thy sisters.

AGAVE.

Fearfully, fearfully, this deep disgrace,
Hath Dionysus brought upon our race.

DIONYSUS.

Fearful on me the wrong that ye had done;
Unhonoured was my name in Thebes alone.

AGAVE.

Father, farewell.

CADMUS.

                    Farewell, my wretched daughter!

AGAVE.

So lead me forth—my sisters now to meet,
Sad fallen exiles.
                      Let me, let me go,
Where cursed Cithæron ne'er may see me more,
Nor I the cursed Cithæron see again.
Where there's no memory of the thyrsus dance.
The Bacchic Orgies be the care of others.

MISCELLANEOUS.

FRAGMENTS FROM THE LYRIC POETS.

TIME and barbarism have hardly inflicted a heavier loss to the man of letters and the lovers of poetry, than that of the Lyric Songs of Greece. So exquisite are the few fragments which remain that the scholar cannot read them without melancholy, from his unavailing regret that they are so rare and so imperfect.

Even of Pindar specimens from only one class of his rich and various poems have come down to us. Of his Hymns (ὕμνοι); his Pæans; his Dithyrambics, the great object of wonder and admiration; his dirges (θρῆνοι); his processional odes chanted by mingled choirs (προσόδια); his Partheneia chanted by maidens; his songs accompanied with dancing (ὑπορχήματα); his drinking songs (σκολιά); his panegyrical odes (ἐγκώμια); not one survives. The Ἐπινίκια (the triumphal odes at the Games) alone remain.

Of these odes we have one excellent translation—that of Carey; and some passages by Abraham Moore show great power and very accomplished scholarship.

Among the fragments, however, of the lost Lyrics, are three or four, not only of great beauty but of singular interest: one the opening of a Dithyramb; one from a dirge, showing the poet's faith in the life of the blessed; one the effect of an eclipse on the religious mind of an early Greek; one recently recovered, on the origin of mankind, the assertion of the proud autocthonism of Greece.

FRAGMENTS FROM THE LYRIC POETS.

Fragment I.

Δεῦτ' ἐς χορὸν 'Ολύμπιοι.

Lords of Olympus, to the hymn come down
Ye Gods, and send to earth your heavenly grace.
    Ye that in Athens' holy town,
In its thronged centre, where rich incense breathes,
Walk in the splendid Forum's sunbright space!
The offering of our violet-twisted wreaths
Receive, all plucked in the sweet hour of Spring.
    Lo, Jove-inspired, in all my pride I sing
    My second hymn to that bright youth divine,
    Whose brows the ivy garlands twine,
Whom mortals Bromius call, the loud-voiced god of wine.
Son of the mightiest Sire, we sing to thee,
And, blest o'er women, Theban Semele!

    In Argive Nemea's field
'Scapes not the poets ardent gaze
    The earliest shoot the palm-tree yields,
As opening wide the chamber of the Hours,

The nectar-breathing flowers
Listen the fragrant Spring's awakening lays.
    Then wide are scattered round,
    O'er all the ambrosial ground,
  The purple violet's blossoms rare,
And roses to be wreathed in maidens' hair.
    Shout, to the pipes uplift the choral song.
    Shout to crowned Semele, ye choral throng.

Fragment II.

Τοῖσι λάμπει μένος ἀελίου.

To them the Sun, in radiant might,
Lights up the subterranean night.
In meads empurpled o'er with roses,
They take their calm suburban ease,
While over them the fragrant shade reposes,
Where golden fruits weigh down the loaded trees.
Some in the chariot's rapid flight,
Some with the dice indulge, or the harp's soft delight.
And still luxuriant all around
The universal plenty blooms,
And over all the holy ground
Float evermore the incense-fumes,
Where from the altars of the gods arise
The far-seen fires of constant sacrifice.

Fragment III.—An Eclipse of the Sun.

'Ακτὶs ἀελίου πολύσκοπε.

O WHY, thou Sun, with thine all-seeing ray
  Beyond the range of mortal sight afar,
    Sovereign of every star,
Robb'st thou the world, even at the noon of day;
  And makest darkling man in vain desire
  The guiding light of thy intolerable fire?
Why, wandering down the dark unwonted way,
    In darkness drives thy car?
  By greatest Jove I supplicate,
    To Thebes' exalted state,
  Urge undisastrous thy fleet steeds divine!
  O noblest! O thou universal sign!
  Some bloody war dost thou presage,
Or withered harvest sad, or tempest's blasting rage?
  Or cruel strife destroying wide?
    Or inroad of the ocean-tide
    Over the peaceful plain?
  Or wintry frosts, or summer rain
  In torrent deluge sweeping down the vale,
To force from all our youth the wild and general wail?

THE ORIGIN OF MAN.

From the Philosophoumena of Hippolytus, as corrected by several *Scholars.*

Πρῶτα δὲ γαῖ' ἄνδωκεν τότ' ἐνεγκαμένα καλὸν γέρας.

END OF STROPHE.

  First bare the Earth
  Man, her majestic birth,
Rejoicing that to her was given the grace
To be the mother of that gentle race
Beloved of heaven! But hard it is to know

ANTISTROPHE.

Whether within the deep Bœotian glen,
  On clear Cephisus' strand,
Rose Alalcomeneus, the first of men;
  Or the Kouretæ upon Ida's side
That race divine; or, yet more old,
  Did first the sun behold
The Corybantes in the Phrygian land
Spring up, like trees, in beauty and in pride?
Did first Arcadia her Pelasgus bear,
  Pelasgus, elder than the moon?
Or hoar Eleusis bear her mystic son,
  Diaulos, in the Rarian haunts to dwell?

Or Lemnos, that bright boy so fair,
  Cabeiros, him, the sire
Of the dark orgies which no tongue may tell?
  Or earlier, bare Pallene rude
  Alcyoneus, nursed in Phlegrean fire,
The eldest of the huge-limbed giant brood?

EPODE.

Nor less doth Libya boast, that first of all
  From her parched plains did strong Iarbas rise,
The acorn fruits from her own tree that fall
  Unto great Jove to bring, sweet sacrifice!
Nilus in Egypt still, as in old time,
  Under her genial influence, moist and warm,
To embodied life her rich prolific slime
  Kindles and quickens into human form.

BACCHYLIDES.

E Scholiis—Vide Bacchylidis Fragmenta a Neue, p. 40.

Γλυκεῖ᾿ ἀνάγκα σευομένα κυλίκων.

How soothing to the enamoured sense
Wine's delicious violence!
Mingling still with Bacchus' gifts,
Hope the kindling mind uplifts.
He that drinks, to empty air
Scatters all his weight of care.
Loftiest cities, turret-crowned,
He can level with the ground.
Universal monarch, he
Reigns in blameless tyranny.
Gold and ivory's gleaming white
Deck his fantastic palace bright.
Laden ships with Egypt's grain
Waft him o'er the glassy main.
Boundless wealth—such visions still
The happy drunkard's bosom fill.

E Pœanibus—Neue, p. 19.

Τίκτει δέ τε θνατοῖσιν Εἰρήνα μεγάλα.

WHAT blessings, Peace! are thine:
    Wealth and the flowers of song
    From many a poet's honied tongue!
On every high-wrought shrine
Blaze in the yellow light the thighs
Of bulls and rich-fleeced flocks in solemn sacrifice.
    Youths crowd the arena's sacred ground,
Where ring the fifes and pipes with jocund din,
    And in the bucklers' clasps, with iron bound,
    Their webs the dusky spiders spin;
And rust subdues the trenchant sword and spear;
Nor more the clarion's brazen voice we hear;
Nor, exiled from the eyes, does sleep depart—
The gentle sleep that soothes the inmost heart.

SIMONIDES.

Ὅτε λάρνακι ἐν δαιδαλέᾳ ἄνεμος.—Gaisford, p. 360.

WHEN rude around the high-wrought ark
The tempests raged, the waters dark
Around the mother tossed and swelled;
With not unmoistened cheek, she held
Her Perseus in her arms, and said:
"What sorrows bow this hapless head!
Thou sleep'st the while, thy gentle breast
Is heaving in unbroken rest;
In this our dark unjoyous home,
Clamped with the rugged brass, the gloom
Scarce broken by the doubtful light
That gleams from yon dim fires of night.
But thou, unwet thy clustering hair,
 Heed'st not the billows raging wild,
The moanings of the bitter air,
 Wrapt in thy purple robe, my beauteous child!
Oh, seemed this peril perilous to thee,
 How sadly to my words of fear.
 Wouldst thou bend down thy listening ear!
But now sleep on, my child! sleep thou, wide sea!
 Sleep, my unutterable agony!
O change thy counsels, Jove, our sorrows end!
And if my rash intemperate zeal offend,
For my child's sake, her father, pardon me!"

THE TOMB OF ANACREON.

The festive gaiety of the following contrasts singularly with the exquisite pathos of the last, the most perfect and inimitable fragment of this kind of Greek lyric poetry.

Ἡμερὶ πανθέλκτειρα.—Gaisford, p. 376.

MOTHER of purple grapes, soul-soothing Vine,
Whose verdant boughs their graceful tendrils twine:
Still round this urn, with youth unfading, bloom,
The gentle slope of old Anacreon's tomb.
For so the unmixed-goblet-loving sire,
Touching the livelong night his amorous lyre,
Even low in earth, upon his brows shall wear
The ruddy clustering crowns thy branches bear,
Where, though still fall the sweetest dews, the song
Distilled more sweetly from that old man's tongue.

EPITAPHIA.

Gaisford, p. 390; *attributed also to Callimachus.*—Blomfield, p. 70.

Ἡ γρῆυς Νικώ.

OLD Nico crowned the young Melittes' tomb,
The virgins'! Death, was this a righteous doom?

Σῆμα καταφθιμένοιο Μεγακλέος.—Gaisford, p. 355.

WHEN thus the tomb of Megacles I see,
O wretched Kallias! how I pity thee!

FRAGMENTS FROM THE ELEGIAC POETS.

THEOGNIS.

Gaisford.—*Poetæ Minores Græci*, p. 254.

Σοὶ μὲν ἐγὼ πτέρ' ἔδωκα.

I GAVE thee wings in easy flight to glide
High o'er all earth and ocean's boundless tide.
Banquet and feast thy presence shall prolong,
The noble theme of every rapturous tongue.
Youths in sweet concord to the shrill-toned fife
Shall chant in measured strain thy glorious life;
And when thy ghost through earth's dark womb shall go
To the wide-wailing realm of Dis below,
In death thou shalt not lose thy failing fame,
But live 'mong men an everlasting name;
O Cyrnus, spread o'er all the Helladian land,
Each wave-washed isle, and ocean's utmost strand.
Not on the trampling courser's back, but swift
Borne by the violet-crownèd Muses' gift;
The theme of song to every future race,
While earth and sun maintain their constant place.
But slight to me thy cold regard, beguiled
By thy soft falsehood, like a humoured child.

Τέρπεό μοι φίλε θυμέ.—Pp. 264, 269.

This Fragment is composed of several thrown together.

TAKE thy delight, my soul! another day
Another race shall see, and I be breathless clay.
Vain mortals, and unwise! who mourn the hour
Of death, not that of youth's departing flower.
For all, whom once the earth hath covered o'er,
Gone down to Erebus' unjoyous shore,
Delight no more to hear the lyre's soft sound,
Nor pass the jocund cups of Bacchus round.
So thou, my soul, shalt revel at thy will,
While light is yet my hand, my head untrembling still.

These fragments were translated long before the *Theognis Restitutus* of Mr. Hookham Frere reached England. In the *Quarterly Review* (vol. lxvii.), I endeavoured to do justice to that admirable and original piece of classical criticism; and in order to make known that which the diffidence or the indolence of Mr. Frere withheld from the public, I quoted from it very largely. The versions were worthy of the translator of Aristophanes and of the Spanish poem of the Cid: I can imagine no higher praise. Of those writers to whom we are indebted for rendering the poems of the classic period, or those of a later age, into English, few have equalled, none have surpassed, Mr. Frere in the happy transmutation of the originals while maintaining their general character.

SOLON.

From Elegy V.—Gaisford, p. 332.

'Ἀλλὰ Ζεὺς πάντων ἐφορᾷ τέλος.

JOVE views the end of all. As sudden burst
Of vernal winds drives off the clouds dispersed,
Heaves the foundations of the billowy deep,
Wastes fertile earth with desolating sweep;
Then mounts to heaven, the abode of deity,
And gives to view the calm and spotless sky;
Beams in his strength the sun through boundless space,
And not a cloud deforms heaven's azure face.

Gaisford, p. 337.

Ἡμετέρη δὲ πόλις κατὰ μὲν Διὸς οὔ ποτ' ὀλεῖται, etc.

NE'ER shall our city fall by doom of Jove,
Or sentence of the immortal powers above,
So strong the high-born ruler of the land,
Pallas Athene, lifts her guardian hand.
But thine own sons, O Athens, are thy fate,
And, slaves to gain, destroy the unconquered state.
Fierce demagogues unjust, o'er whom shall flow,
For their dark crimes, a bitter tide of woe;
Whose pampered wills brook no restraint, nor rest,
Enjoying, with calm hearts, good fortune's feast.

FRAGMENTS FROM THE TRAGEDIANS.

ÆSCHYLUS.

Prometheus Vinctus, 115-118—124-126.   Edit. Blomfield.

Τίς ἀχώ; τίς ὀδμὰ προσέπτα μ' ἀφεγγής;

WHAT sound, what viewless odour floats around,
    Divine or mortal, or of mingled race?
Come ye to earth's remotest bound
    Spectators on my woes to gaze?

*   *   *   *

Alas! alas! more near, more near,
The winnowing plumes of birds I hear;
All the air around me rings,
With motion light of fluttering wings.

sub finem 1079.

πρὸς ταῦτ' ἐπ' ἐμοί.

Aye on that head the lightnings hurl
In sharp-edged flakes that blaze and curl!
With thunders rend the shivering heaven,
And blasts in frantic eddies driven!
The earth, to its foundations bare,
Up from its roots let whirlwinds tear!

Confound wild ocean in its wrath
Even with heaven's stars in their empyreal path:
   And let him hurl amid the storm,
   Deep, deep to Tartarus, my form;
   Plunged in the gulf of dark Necessity;
   Yet never never can he make me die!

l. 116.

   And now in deed, no more in word,
   The rockings of the earth I heard;
   Hark the long thunder's bellowing sound!
   Volumes of lightning blaze around;
   Fierce hurricanes roll the cloudy dust,
   Forth leaps each wind, with roaring gust
   Meeting in furious enmity;
   Confusion mingles sea and sky;
   So wild a blast and full of dread
From Jove pours manifest upon my blameless head.
   O, my great mother's holiness!
O Heaven! that giv'st thy common light to bless
   All human-kind, look down and see
   The black injustice of my misery!

THE EUMENIDES.—SONG OF THE FURIES.

Ἄγε δὴ καὶ χορὸν ἅψωμεν. L. 302, Edit. Schütz.

Up and lead the dance of Fate!
Lift the song that mortals hate!
Tell what rights **are** ours on earth,
Over all of human birth.
Swift of foot t' avenge are we!
    He whose hands are clean and pure,
Nought our wrath to dread hath he;
    Calm his cloudless days endure.

But the man that seeks to hide
   Like him,* his gore-bedewèd hands,
Witnesses to them that died,
The blood avengers at his side,
   The Furies' troop for ever stands.

   Mother! that us thy sacred brood didst bear!
      O mother Night!
Us, owned by all—the blind to earthly light,
And those that yet behold Heaven's sunshine bright,
   The Powers of vengeance, hear!
      See us dishonoured by Latona's son,
         Who far hath rent away
         This our devoted prey,
   For deed of murder on his mother done.

   O'er our victim come begin!
      Come, the incantation sing,
      Frantic all and maddening,
   To the heart a brand of fire,
      The Furies' hymn,
   That which chains the senses dim,
   Tuneless to the gentle lyre,
      Withering the soul within.

   Even at our birth the Fates decreed,
   To us the everlasting meed;

* Orestes.

Whoe'er untimely blood hath spilt,
Loading his soul with murtherous guilt;
His restless followers still to be,
Even till he refuge take beneath
The darksome earth, nor yet in death
From our inevitable presence free.

O'er our victim come begin!
Come the incantation sing
Frantic all and maddening,
To the heart a brand of fire,
The Furies' hymn.
That which chains the senses dim,
Tuneless to the gentle lyre,
Withering the soul within.

Such at our birth our lot was given,
Ne'er to approach the immortal Gods of heaven,
Nor ever at the joyous feast
Was deity of light our guest,
Nor share nor portion e'er had we
In the white robes of their festivity.

We the task of ruin chose,
T' o'erthrow the palaces of those
Who in the bloody civil strife
Stain their hands with kindred life.
Him our restless feet pursue;
In his triumphant hour,

And while the reeking blood is new,
  We crush him in his power.

We thus the weight of care remove
  From the great avenging Jove.
Thus men of blood our imprecations free
  From judgment of each other deity;
  For highest Jove this hateful race
Forbids to stand before his awful face.

The pride of all of human birth,
  All glorious in the eye of day,
  Dishonoured slowly melts away,
Trod down and trampled to the earth,
Whene'er our dark-stoled troop advances,
Whene'er our feet lead on the dismal dances.

For leaping down from high, I place
  My stern foot's ponderous weight,
Supplanting him in his triumphant race,
And hurling him down headlong—awful fate!
He whom the darkness of his guilt o'erclouds
  In sin's blind dulness still the doom defies,
Till through the gloom his fated house that shrouds,
  Wail feebly forth the many-voicèd cries.

For light our footsteps are,
  And perfect is our might,
Awful remembrancers of guilt and crime,

    Implacable to mortal prayer,
Far from the gods, unhonoured, and heaven's light,
    We hold our voiceless dwellings dread,
All unapproached by living or by dead.

    What mortal feels not awe,
  Nor trembles at our name,
Hearing our fate-appointed power sublime,
    Fixed by the eternal law.
For old our office, and our fame,
    Might never yet of its due honours fail,
Though 'neath the earth our realm in unsunn'd regions pale.

CHORUS FROM THE ἹΚΕΤΙΔΕΣ.

L. 540. Edit. Schütz.*

'Ἄναξ ἀνάκτων.

O KING of kings! all wealthiest Jove!
Blest beyond all the blest above!
O'er all the mightiest, mightiest thou,
Hear and accord our solemn vow.
Arise, and in thy righteous hate
  O'erwhelm our foes' insulting pride,
  And deep in ocean's purple tide
Plunge thou the black-oared bark of Fate.

Our suppliant female troop behold
Sprung from that famous lineage old,
By her of yore beloved by thee.
(Recall her pleasing history)
Fair Io's paramour divine,
  Forget not thou thy amorous flame!
  From Jove our high descent we claim
This land the mother of our line.

For here, returning to our home,
O'er old forgotten tracks we roam,
Along our mother's favourite mead
Whose flowers the browsing heifers feed,

---

* This chorus was translated at the request of that singularly acute and elegant scholar, Peter Elmsley, who had expressed high praise—rare with him—of some of the former translations.

Whence Io rushed all maddening
Before the hornets' goading sting.
Through countless nations on she went,
Right through the severed continent;
Twice Europe's bounding straits she passed,
And stood upon the wave-washed shore at last.

On Asia's coast she swift arrives,
Fast through the Phrygian pastures drives;
And on by Teuthras' Mysian town
In Lydia's glens she plunges down:
O'er rough Cilicia's cliffs she ran;
Through every wild Pamphylian clan;
O'er many a river still she fled,
Deep in its everlasting bed:
To the rich land at length she roves,
The corn-clad isle that Aphrodite loves.

And still transfixed with th' arrowy sting
Of that fierce herdsman on the wing,
She reached Jove's fertile grove at length,
Where Typhon rushes in his strength:
Meads, ever fed with melting snows,
Where Nilus' healthful water flows,
Whose shores disease may never taint;
There, with unseemly labours faint,
She sank beneath the sting of fire,
By Herè sent in her remorseless ire.

Round the dread stranger, pale with fear,
The people of the land drew near,
And saw, with palpitating breast,
The mingled form of man and beast,
Heifer and woman! in amaze
On that prodigious form they gaze.
And who was he that soothed to rest
That weary wandering maid distrest,
Sad Io, o'er her endless road,
Driven by the hornets' unrelenting goad?

 The King of the eternal ages,
 Jove himself her grief assuages.
Beneath th' unharming power she lay,
 And heaven-breathed quiet lulled her frame,
And in soft tears distilled away
  Her sorrow and her shame.
The burthen of her innocence beguiled,
Ere long she bore to light the blameless child.

 From age to age endured his glory;
  All the earth rang with his story.
And hence from him, the Lord of life,
 We trace our line, great Jove our sire;
Who else could end the wondrous strife
  Of Herè's raging ire?
 Great Jove's the deed, and so we trace
To Epaphus of right our heaven-born race.

208 FRAGMENTS FROM THE TRAGEDIANS.

Whom call we of the powers above
Our righteous cause most fitly to protect?
   The sire that planted all our land,
   The King with the omnipotent right hand,
Our race's ancient mighty architect,
   The all-defending, the propitious Jove.

   Nor subject e'er to others sway,
Nor less than greatest was his sovereign state;
   To none upraised on loftier throne
   Was ever all-submissive homage shown.
Deeds on his sovereign word for ever wait,
   The counsels of his mind brook no delay.

SOPHOCLES.

I made but few translations from Sophocles—the most perfect of the Greek Tragic writers—on account of his perfection. The transcendent excellence of Sophocles is in his conception of Tragedy, either as a single play, or in a Trilogy like the Œdipodean. His style, too, from its fine harmony between the thought and the language, baffles translation more than his less equable rivals, who are great in insulated passages, and in what I will venture to call more eccentric poetic language.

The two speeches which follow are from the "Antigone," which have an exquisite pathos to my ear, even surpassing Euripides in his most tender moods.

ANTIGONE.

'Ορᾶτε μ' ὦ γᾶς πατρίας πολῖται.—L. 806.   Edit. Brunck.

Come, fellow-citizens, and see
The desolate Antigone,
On the last path her steps shall tread,
Set forth, the journey of the dead:
Watching, with vainly-lingering gaze,
Her last, last sun's expiring rays;
Never to see it, never more!
For down to Acheron's dread shore
A living victim am I led
To Hades' universal bed.

> To my dark lot no bridal joys
> Belong, nor e'er the jocund noise
> Of hymenæan chant shall sound for me;
> But Death, cold Death my only spouse shall be.

Ibid.—οἴ μοι γελῶμαι.—L. **838**.

> Ah me! and am I laughed to scorn?
> Oh! by my country's Gods I pray,
> Why mock ye me, not yet to burial borne,
> But living in the light of day.

> Thou city, hear my call!
> And ye the city's wealthy burghers all!
> Alas! sweet Dirce's fountain stream,
> And Thebes's grove, where the bright chariots gleam,
> Bear witness to my dreary lot.
> How, by my treacherous friends unwept, forgot,
> I go, obedient to my doom,
> To the dark dungeon of this new-heaped tomb.
> O miserable me!
> Nor with the living nor the dead to be!
> But in lone banishment to lie,
> Where man may neither live, nor yet may die.
> Unmourned, unfriended, and unwed,
> My dismal journey am I led:
> No more may I behold the eye
> Of that great holy lamp on high;
> And o'er my tearless grave shall moan
> Of all my reckless friends not one.

O tomb! O bridal chamber! O deep-delved
And strongly-guarded mansion! I descend
To meet in your dread chambers all my kindred,
Who in dark multitudes have crowded down
Where Proserpine receives the dead. But I,
The last—and oh, how few more miserable!—
Go down, or ere my sands of life are run.

EURIPIDES.

The depreciation, almost contemptuous, of Euripides seems to be an axiom of modern criticism. The disparaging judgment of A. W. Schlegel, and the scornful sentence of Macaulay (who, however, as I have said, fully admitted the excellence of his "Bacchæ"), may seem to have determined the question. Yet I must confess my sympathy with Mr. Coleridge, who speaks with his peculiar warmth of the "passionate outpourings" of Euripides; and the greater than Coleridge—Milton—who seems to have had a passion for "Sad Electra's Poet." Perhaps their beauty is heightened when read as separate poetic passages, by their independence of the dramatic action. Hence to me the charm of the Troades. It is no drama, it has scarcely a fable. It is a series of pathetic speeches and exquisite odes on the fall of Troy. What can be more admirable, in the midst of all these speeches of woe and sorrow, than the wild outburst of Cassandra into a bridal song, instead of, as Shakespeare describes her, "shrilling her dolours forth?"

CASSANDRA.

Ἄνεχε, πάρεχε φῶς, φέρε.—L. 310. Ed. Matthiæ.

A LIGHT! a light! rise up, be swift;
I seize, I worship, and I lift
The bridal torches' festal rays,
Till all the burning fane's ablaze!
    Hymen! Hymenæan king!
Look there! look there! what blessings wait
Upon the bridegroom's nuptial state!
And I, how blest, who proudly ride
Through Argos' streets, a queenly bride!
    Go thou, my mother! go!
    With many a gushing tear
    And frantic shriek of woe.

Wail for thy sire, thy country dear!
  I the while, in bridal glee,
    Lift the glowing, glittering fire.
Hymen! Hymen! all to thee
    Flames the torch and rings the lyre!
Bless, O Hecate, the rite;
Send thy soft and holy light
To the virgin's nuptial bed.
Lightly lift the airy tread!
Evan! Evan! dance along!
Holy are the dance and song.
Meetest they to celebrate
My father Priam's blissful fate.
  Dance, O Phœbus, dance and sing!
    Round thy laurel-shaded fane
    Still I lead the priestess' train.
Hymen! Hymenæan king!
Dance, my mother, lift thy feet!
  Here and there the cadence keep
  With thy light and frolic step!
Sing the Hymenæan sweet,
  With many a gladsome melody
  And jocund nymph's exultant cry.
Beauteous-vested maids of Troy,
  Sing my song of nuptial joy!
  Sing the fated husband led
To my virgin bridal-bed.

TROADES.

Ἀμφί μοι Ἴλιον, ὦ Μοῦσα.—L. 515.

A SAD unwonted song,
O'er Ilion, Muse, prolong,
Mingled with tears of woe,
The funeral anthem slow.

I too, with shriek and frantic cry,
Take up that dismal melody,
Through that ill-omened four-wheeled car,
A captive to the Argive war;
What time the Greek, or ere he fled,
Left at our gate that armed steed,
Menacing the heavens with giant height,
And all with golden housings glittering bright.

Shouted all the people loud,
On the rock-built height that stood,
" Come," they sang, as on they prest,
" Come, from all our toil releas'd,

Lead the blest image to the shrine
Of her the Jove-born Trojan maid divine."

Lingered then no timorous maid,
Nor age his tardy steps delayed:
With gladsome shout and jocund song
They led their treacherous fate along.
All at once the Phrygian rout
From the bursting gates rushed out;
On the dangerous gift they lead,
The beauty of the unyoked immortal steed,

With its ambushed warriors freight,
Argos' pride, and Ilion's fate.
Round the stately horse, and round
Cord and cable soon they wound,
And drag it on, like pinnace dark
Of some tall and gallant bark,
To the temple's marble floor,
Too soon to swim with reeking Trojan gore.

O'er the toil, the triumph spread
Silent night her curtained shade,
But Lybian fifes still sweetly rang,
And many a Phrygian air they sang,
And maidens danced with airy feet,
To the jocund measures sweet;

And every home was blazing bright,
  As the glowing festal light
Its rich and purple splendour streamed,
Where high and full the mantling wine-cup gleamed.

But I the while the palace courts around,
  Hymning the mountain-queen, Jove's virgin daughter,
Went, with blithe dance and music's sprightly sound—
  When all at once the frantic cry of slaughter,
Throughout the wide and startled city ran ;
  The cowering infants on their mothers' breasts,
  Folded their trembling hands within her vests—
Forth stalked the ambushed Mars, and his fell work began—

  The work of Pallas in her ire.
  Then round each waning altar fire,
  Wild Carnage, drunk with Phrygian blood,
  And murtherous Desolation, strew'd
  Where, in her couch of slumber, laid,
  Was wont to rest the tender maid ;
  To Greece the crown of triumph gave,
And crown'd the cup of woe to each sad Phrygian slave.

TROADES.

The lamentation of Hecuba over the dead body of Astyanax, cast down from the walls of Troy.—Δύστηνε κρατός.—L. 1193.

O BEAUTIFUL but most ill-fated head!
How miserably have your native walls,
The towers Apollo built, shorn thy bright honours!
The rich luxuriant hairs thy mother cherished,
Like garden flowers, imprinting many a kiss.
There now, through the crushed bone, the blood
  gleams out.
No more of this—O delicate hands, relaxed
In each stiff joint, ye lie before me! Lips
That used in sportive boastfulness to soothe me!
Thou hast perished! thou hast played me false!
  While close
I folded thee within my robes, "Dear grandame,"
Thou saidst, "How many a lock of this rich hair
I'll pluck to strew thy tomb, and lead about
Thy funeral dance." Ah, dear deceitful language!
Not at my burial thou, but I at thine,
Old, houseless, childless, fold thy corpse—Ah me!
The fond embraces, those sweet nursery cares,
Those gentle slumbers wasted all, and vain!

ION.

The "Ion" of Euripides is to me a charming play. The opening scene of the boy employed in scaring the birds from the temple of Apollo—a sort of young pagan Acolyth—is full of grace and fancy.

ἔα, ἔα, φοιτῶσ' ἤδη, λείπουσίν τε.—L. 154.

BEHOLD! behold!
Now they come, they quit the nest
On Parnassus' topmost crest.
Hence! away! I warn ye all!
Light not on our hallowed wall!
From eave and cornice keep aloof,
And from the golden gleaming roof!
Herald of Jove! of birds the king!
Fierce of talon, strong of wing,
Hence! begone! or thou shalt know
The terrors of this deadly bow.
Lo! where rich the altar fumes,
Soars yon swan on oary plumes.
Hence, and quiver in thy flight
Thy foot that gleams with purple light,
Even though Phœbus' harp rejoice
To mingle with thy tuneful voice;
Far away thy white wings shake
O'er the silver Delian lake.

Hence! obey! or end in blood
The music of thy sweet-voiced ode.

Away! away! another stoops!
Down his flagging pinion droops,
Shall our marble eaves be hung
With straw nests for your callow young?
Hence, or dread this twanging bow,
Hence, where Alpheus' waters flow,
Or the Isthmian groves among
Go and rear your nestling young.
Hence, nor dare pollute or stain
Phœbus' offerings, Phœbus' fane.
Yet I feel a sacred dread,
Lest your scattered plumes I shed;
Holy birds! 'tis yours to show
Heaven's auguries to men below.

FRAGMENTS FROM THE COMEDY.

ARISTOPHANES.

ΠΑΡΑΒΑΣΙΣ—FROM "THE PEACE."

My translations from Aristophanes were few, fortunately. Mr. Frere had only begun, or only partially imparted to the public, his unrivalled versions of the great Attic comic poet. I had ventured only one or two short speeches; and two passages of that exquisite Attic grace and melody, in which that wonderful master of the broadest comic humour and the most cutting satire surpassed the sweetest and most musical of his more serious rivals.

εἰ δ' οὖν εἰκὸς τινα τιμῆσαι.—l. 736. Edit. Dindorf.

BE honour given where honour's due: our poet stands confest
Of all our comic teachers—the wisest and the best.
For he alone, with nobler aim—his rivals made to cease,
On rags for ever jesting—and waging war on fleas.
Still making poor starved Hercules—like a glutton munch and eat;
And now a runaway and rogue—and ever soundly beat.
All these, dishonoured, from your stage—he drove away and gave
A truce to that eternal flogged—and ever howling slave;
While evermore his brother slave—would o'er his stripes begin
His sorry jests—"Poor fellow! what's—the matter with your skin?

Alas! and has the bristly whip—thus ventured to attack
Thy sides with his fierce legions—and thus laid waste
    thy back?"
This wretched burthen off he threw—this low-born
    ribaldry;
Created you a noble art—and set it up on high,
With lofty words and sentences—disdaining as unfit
Women and petty private men—for his unvulgar wit.
At once upon the highest with—Herculean strength I
    sprung,
Through stench of filthiest tan-hides—and pelting showers
    of dung;
And first that blatant beast I fought—with sharpest
    teeth o'ergrown,
Whose fiery eyes more fierce than those—of shameless
    Cinna shone.
And all around his brows the heads—of sycophants
    were hung,
That rolled out o'er his noisome cheek—the flattering,
    slavering tongue.
And torrent-like his voice poured forth—fierce ruin un-
    represt,
With all the mingled filth and stench—of every loath-
    some beast.
Against this dreadful monster I—feared not alone t'
    arise,
In your defence, my countrymen!—and the Islands our
    allies.

FROM "THE BIRDS."

TO THE NIGHTINGALE.

Ἄγε σύννομέ μοι, παῦσαι μὲν ὕπνου.—L. 209. Edit. Dindorf.

SISTER warbler, cease from slumber,
Pour thy sweetest holiest number;
With thy heavenly voice bewail
Thy own sad Itys' tearful tale;
Gushing forth the liquid note
Copious through thy yellow throat.
Clear and full the holy sound,
Through the full-leaved ivy round,
Soars away to Jove's high hall:
Gold-haired Phœbus hears the call;
Hears and answers back again,
Mournful to the mournful strain.
He with ivory-gleaming lyre
Wakens all the immortal choir,
    All the everlasting throng
      Take up the song,
The voices of the blest the full accord prolong.

FROM "THE CLOUDS."

The Invocation—ὦ δέσποτ' ἄναξ.—L. 264.

SOCRATES.

O Lord and King, unmeasured Air—that bearest up on high
This vast and floating world sublime—and thou, O glorious Sky!
And ye, O thunder-flashing Clouds—mysterious deities!
Arise! appear! great Queens, aloft—before the sage, arise!

STREPSIADES.

Not yet, before I wrap me close—lest I be drenched with wet:
Ah me! my bonnet's left at home—Beseech ye, sirs, not yet.

SOCRATES.

Arise! all-honoured Clouds arise!—your gorgeous muster show!
Where'er you haunt, Olympus' brow—beat with eternal snow;
Or in his garden groves ye dance—with father Ocean's daughters;
Or with your golden wings ye draw—dark Nilus' fountain waters;

Brood o'er the slow Mœotis lake—or Mimas' summit
    drear;
Receive our costly sacrifice—our solemn summons hear!

THE CLOUDS.

We come! we come!
The Eternal Clouds, to mortal sight,
Our dewy forms are floating light,
From father Ocean's ever-sounding home,
Up to the loftiest mountain's wood-capt brow;
    Whence on the beaconing watch-towers bright,
    Down we cast our ranging sight;
    Where the rich champain spreads below,
  And where the murmuring rivers pour,
And the deep endless seas for ever roar.

    For lo, the unwearied eye
    Of heaven is blazing high,
Bathing all nature in its glittering beams;
    Our dripping mists we shake away,
    In our immortal forms survey,
Where to the expanding ken the world of glory gleams.

FROM "PHILEMON."

Cumberland, in the *Observer*, gave an excellent translation of most of the fragments of the later comic writers. Poor Cumberland! What he wrote, which was worthy of memory, is forgotten, while he lives as Sir Fretful Plagiary.

The following are a few which escaped Cumberland.

Νὴ τὸν Δία τὸν μέγιστον, ᾤμην, Σωσία.—P. 843. Edit. Meineke.

Now by great Jove! I deemed of old, my Sosia,
The poor alone dragged out their weary lives
In one dark perpetuity of sorrow;
But smooth and easy flowed the jocund days
Of wealthy men. Now wiser, I confess,
Largely to spend is wealth's sole privilege;
The eminent are eminent in wretchedness.

PHILEMON.

ἀνὴρ δίκαιός ἐστιν οὐχ ὁ μὴ ἀδικῶν.

He is not just who doth no wrong, but he
Who will not when he may; not he who, lured
By some poor petty prize, abstains, but he
Who with some mighty treasure in his grasp
May sin securely, yet abhors the sin.
Not he who closely skirts the pale of law,
But he whose generous nature, void of guile—
Would be, not seem to be, the upright man.

THE SKOLIA.

The σκόλια may be described as the popular songs of Greece. We have several—some in my judgment of remarkable grace and beauty. They have been collected in a small volume by Ilgen. One or two more—that of the swallow—are preserved in Athenæus. I begin with that which was dearest to the popular ear in Athens—the "God save the King" of the Republic.

'Εν μύρτου κλαδί.

In myrtle wreath my sword I sheathe,
   Thus his brand Harmodius drew;
   Thus Aristogiton slew
The tyrant lord in freedom's cause,
And gave to Athens equal laws.

In myrtle wreath my sword I sheathe,
   Thus his brand Harmodius drew;
   Thus Aristogiton slew,
When Athens' holiest festival
Beheld the tyrant lord, Hipparchus, fall.

In deathless fame thy living name,
   Harmodius! shall for ever shine,
   And, brave Aristogiton! thine,
Who struck the blow in freedom's cause,
And gave to Athens equal laws.

Thou art not dead, thy spirit fled,
  Harmodius! to its sacred rest,
  Among the islands of the blest;
Where the swift-footed Peleus' son, they tell,
And godlike Diomede for ever dwell.

The following may be called Religious Chants; no doubt formed part of the Temple services.

TO PALLAS.

Παλλὰς τριτογένει', ἄνασσ' 'Αθηνᾶ.

O PALLAS, sprung from Jove! Athenian Queen!
Protect this city, and each citizen,
  From war, and civil discord dire,
  And death untimely, thou, and thy dread Sire!

TO CERES.

Πλούτου μῆτερ.—P. 4.

MOTHER of wealth! Olympian! Thee we sing
Ceres, when the glad Hours the garlands bring,
  And thou, all hail! Jove's seed divine!
  Guard well this city, awful Proserpine!

TO APOLLO AND ARTEMIS.

'Εν Δήλῳ.—P. 7.

Of old in Delos did Latona bear
Her twins—King Phœbus with the golden hair,
  The Huntress Queen, the deer who slays,
  Artemis, whom all womankind obeys.

TO PAN.

'Ιὼ Πάν.—P. 10.

Ho, Pan, the famed Arcadian sovereign,
Dancing with the light Nymphs in Bacchus' train,
  Ho, Pan! with all thy jocund throng,
  Smile on the rapture of our festive song.

SONG.

Εἴθε λύρα καλὴ γενοίμην.—P. 32.

I would I were a beauteous ivory lyre,
  And me the beauteous youth should bear
    In Bacchus' festal choir!

And I a golden urn unstained by fire,
  And me some beauteous maid should bear,
    Holy and chaste as fair.

SONGS OF COMMON LIFE.

THE SOLDIER'S SONG.

Ἔστι μοι πλοῦτος μέγας δόρυ.

This is my wealth, the sword I wield,
My spear, my buckler, and my shield.
With these I plough, with these I reap,
And from the winepress rich and deep
Trample out the flowing wine,
While hosts of slaves await my sign.
But those the sword who dare not wield,
The spear, the buckler, and the shield,
With bended knee come bow to me,
And call me mighty king, their earthly deity.

THE MAN OF PEACE.

Οὐ βοῶν πάρεστι.—*Bacchylides*, p. 245.

No lowing herds I fold,
Nor heap the sparkling gold,
Nor the soft couch, with purple dyed, is mine;
But the calm equal mind,
And the sweet Muse you'll find,
And in Bœotian cups the generous wine.

CONTEMPT OF WEALTH.

Ὠφελέν σε τυφλὲ Πλοῦτε.—P. 230.

Off! away! blind god of gain!
Nor on shore, nor on the main,
Nor on the steadfast continent,
Thy ill-omened face present.
Off to Tartarus begone,
And thy native Acheron!
Source accurst of every woe
That man inherits here below.

CONVIVIAL SONGS.

Σύν μοι πῖνε.—Ilgen, p. 86.

Drink the glad wine with me,
   With me spend youth's gay hours ;
Or a sighing lover be,
   Or crown thy brow with flowers.
When I am merry and mad,
   Merry and mad be you ;
When I am sober and sad,
   Be sad and sober too.

Οὔ μοι μέλει τὰ Γυγέω.

What is Gyges' wealth to me,
Though golden Sardis' king he be ?
I desire not to be great,
Envy not the tyrant's state.
All my joy is still to wear
Rosy chaplets in my hair.
To-day, to-day's my care alone ;
The dark to-morrow's all unknown.

These sometimes took a more grave and serious cast.

Οὔ μοι τὰ Γυγέω.—Archilochus, p. 183.

No care have I of Gyges' golden store,
Unenvious I for nought the gods implore ;
I have no love of wide and kingly sway,
But turn from pride my reckless eyes away.

'Ανθρώπων ὀλίγον μὲν κάρτος.—P. 229.

VAIN of mortal men the strength,
His life of care a weary length.
All his days so few and brief,
Toil on toil, and grief on grief,
And still, where'er his course he tends,
Inevitable death impends;
And for the worst, and for the best,
Is strewn the same dark couch of rest.

Ὑγιαίνειν μὲν ἄριστον ἀνδρὶ θνατῷ.—P. 25.

THE best of gifts to mortal man is health;
The next the bloom of beauty's matchless flower;
The third is blameless and unfraudful wealth;
The fourth with friends to waste youth's joyous hour.

This will be well followed by the beautiful Ode to Health.

Ὑγίεια πρεσβίστα μακάρων.—P. 120.

O THOU, the first and best
Of the Immortal Blest;
O Health! how gladly would I dwell with thee,
Till my last sands are run,
And my brief life is done,
Come to my home, my willing guest to be!
If there be joy in wealth,
Or soft parental love,
Or the delicious stealth,

With which young Aphrodite winds
Her nets around her captives' willing minds;
Or if aught else of joy the gods bestow,
Or sweet cessation of our toil and woe,
With thee, O blessed Health!
All bloom in one unending spring,
And bliss where thou art not is ever on the wing.

THE SONG OF THE SWALLOW.

From *Athenæus*, viii. 60. ἦλθ', ἦλθε, χελιδών.

THE swallow is come, she is come to bring
The laughing hours of the blithesome spring;
The youth of the year and its sunshine bright,
With her back all dark, and her breast all white.

THE CAROL.

COME like men of wealth and worth,
Bring your luscious fig-cakes forth,
With a little cup of wine,
Or the meal that's white and fine,
With the basket full of cheese;
Or, the swallow would you please—
She is never over-nice—
An omelet's ready in a trice.

Will ye give, or must we go?
Scurvy churls! ye 'scape not so.
Doors and door-posts shall come down,
   Or the pretty wife within,
   That's so small, and light, and thin,
Look ye, in a trice she's gone.
   Give, and give with hearty cheer,
Open, open at our call;
   Old nor sturdy beggars fear,
Merry, merry children, one and all;
Merry, merry boys, we sing and follow,
Blithe in the train of the blithesome swallow.

I am unwilling altogether to omit the specimens which remain of Attic Comic Song. Certainly there is little of what we conceive to be fine Attic wit in this broad burlesque; yet the Greek land of Cockayne is not without interest.

FROM TELECLIDES.

Λέξω τοίνυν βίον ἐξ ἀρχῆς.—*Athenæus*, vi. 95.

HEAR what jocund lives befall
   Mortal men at my command:
Even like water, first of all
   Peace is poured on every hand.
Never bears the bounteous earth,
   Grief, or pain, or slow disease,
But her teeming womb gives birth,
   Instant to whate'er we please.

Every ditch with wine is flowing,
   Loaves and cakes around us fight,
Each our dainty palate wooing,
   Boasting each its purer white.
To our kitchens troop the fish,
   Haste themselves to boil and fry,
Lay them down upon the dish,
   And to the smoking table hie.
Flows of broth a savoury tide,
   Round our couches bubbling still ;
And little rills of sauces glide,
   In smooth meanders, where we will.
Plenteous down the throat they pour,
   Washing down the richest messes.
Dish on dish in endless store,
   Its smoking top with sweetmeats dresses.
Down our throats self-roasted thrushes
   And self-stuffed with pudding fly ;
Jostling cheesecake cheesecake pushes,
   Round our mouths with strife and cry.
For the smoking udder's slice
Little children play at dice.
All grew fat and portly then,
Giants 'mid the sons of men.

THE SAME FROM PHERECRATES.

Athenæus, vi. 97.

Τίς δ' ἔσθ' ἡμῖν τῶν νῦν ἀροτῶν.

WHAT care we for those that plough,
Or those that yoke the bullock now?
Smith nor brazier's art we need,
Trenching ground or scattering seed.
Down our highways, nothing loth,
Rivers flow of savoury broth,
Black and deep, and bubbling o'er,
With mighty cakes that down them pour,
Forth from Plutus' fountains still,
For all to draw and drink their fill.
Jove, whene'er he rains, his showers
Of racy wine, to bathe us, pours;
And from our roofs abundant stream
Grapes, all steeped in clouted cream;
And boiling soup of richest savour,
And roots of choicest highest flavour.
Leaves the mountain trees bear not,
But flesh of birds all piping hot,
And tenderest onions, budding still,
Where the hissing thrushes grill.

POETRY OF THE PHILOSOPHERS.

Several sweet snatches of verse are attributed to Plato; the Attic purity of the verse is worthy of his prose.

Ἄλσος δ' ὡς ἱκόμεσθα βαθύσκιον.—Brunckii Analecta, i. 174.

DEEP in the bosom of the shady grove,
Like purple fruit, lay Cytherea's boy;
Upon the flowering branches idle hung
His bow and crowded quiver. He, embowered
'Mid cups of roses, slumber's captive, slept,
And sleeping smiled, while to and fro the bees
Went hiving sweetest honey from his lips.

Ναυηγοῦ τάφος εἰμί.—Ibid.

HERE lies a sailor, there a peasant swain!
Alike to thee, O Death, the land and main.

Ὑψίκομον παρὰ τάνδε.—i. 172.

COME, and beneath this tall and quivering pine,
That holds sweet converse with the breeze, recline:
And, where the bubbling waters wander by,
My pipe shall win to sleep thy willing eye.

Ἀστέρας εἰσαθρεῖς.—L. 169.

THOU gazest on the stars; were I yon skies,
To look upon thee with a thousand eyes!

THE STATUE OF A SATYR BY A FOUNTAIN-SIDE; LOVE SLEEPING NEAR.

Τὸν Βρομίου Σάτυρον—L. 172.

A SATYR, summoned by the dædal hand,
From the dumb marble, breathing here I stand;
Companion to the fountain Nymphs; no more
The purple wine, the limpid stream I pour.
Light lift thy quiet foot, nor wake the boy,
Who lies dissolved in slumber's blameless joy.

Aristotle's poetry, if this be Aristotle's, is in a loftier moral mood.

TO VIRTUE.

Ἀρετὰ πολύμοχθε.—*Brunckii Analecta*, l. 177.

VIRTUE, laborious good! the noblest spoil
That man can track through the stern paths of duty.
 O Virgin, for thy beauty
To die, or to endure unceasing toil,
 In elder Greece was deemed the fate
 Her noblest sons might emulate.
Such was the harvest in the bounteous soil
Of lofty minds, sown by thy liberal hand,
 Better than gold, or highborn ancestry,
Or the sweet sleep that seals the weary eye.
 For thee the Theban son of Jove,
And Leda's twins with suffering nobly strove,
Thy might proclaiming to each wondering land.

Achilles, burning with desire
> Of thy bright charms, and Ajax trod,
> Untimely, Pluto's drear abode.
> And kindling thus, with fatal fire,

Atarne's nursling, of his might
Widowed too soon the sun's admiring light.
Wherefore his name in loftiest verse
Shall memory's daughters still rehearse,
A sacred name to hospitable Jove,
A glory and a pride to deathless social love.

Fragments only remain—but very remarkable fragments—of the great philosophic poem of Greece, that of Empedocles. It remained for Latin poetry to unfold the atomic theory with a grandeur and power never attained by later Latin verse. The Roman character of Lucretius, with his rich imagination and picturesqueness of language, soars high above the calm didactic tone of the Greek poet, though in him there is enough to show that it maintained all its exquisite pellucid clearness.

Here and there there is a passage which reads like the word-painting of Lucretius:—

ἐχίνοις
ὀξυβελεῖς χαῖται νώτοις ἐπιπεφρίκασι.

The porcupine,
Whose arrowy hairs stand horrent on his back.

Ὦ φίλοι οἳ μέγα ἄστυ.—L. 364. Edit. Sturz.

O FRIENDS, that in your lofty mansions dwell,
Near Agrigentum's rock-built citadel,

Blameless and good, the stranger ne'er implores
In vain before your hospitable doors.
How, as a God, I walk your wondering streets,
Me, as beseems, no mortal homage greets.
With crowns and fillets glittering on my head,
Men, women, gaze and worship where I tread;
And gathering thousands on my footsteps wait.
Some eager ask the dark decrees of fate;
And some the golden path that leads to wealth;
Or powerful words that charm disease to health.

τοῦτον μὲν βροτέων μελέων.—L. 220.

To mould the human body's glorious frame,
At Love's sweet call, each part harmonious came,
Till the full form stood up in perfect life;
Anon disjoined by all-dissolving strife,
When life is ebbing on its utmost shore,
Each separate part goes wandering as of yore.
And thus the trees, the beasts in mountain lair;
Fish in their watery halls, and birds that walk the air.

δίπλ' ἐρέω, τότε μὲν γὰρ ἓν ηὐξήθη.—L. 34.

Now the vast One from mingling myriads grows,
The One dissolved in separate myriads flows.
Thus swift as one is born another fails,
As concord here, and discord there prevails.
From life to death the unwearied atoms range,
And changing still, nor ever cease to change;

Now Love unites each fond harmonious part,
Strife rules: in hate they sever and asunder start.

Πῦρ καὶ Ὕδωρ καὶ Γαῖα.—L. 50.

FIRE, Water, Earth, and Ether's boundless height,
Destroying Strife with these, as infinite,
And Love, in length, depth, vastness unconfined—
Survey them with the eyesight of the mind.
Man may not know that through all being reigns
The power that thrills along his mortal veins;
Whence kindred hearts with mutual kindness glow,
Or Joy or Venus is its name below.
These elemental forms by her control
Melt into form, become the living Whole.
These four, in age, extent, and power the same,
Each hath its instinct, each its share of fame;
For each in turn prevails, as time rolls on
These still are born and die, and these alone.
Were they extinct, existence then must cease;
Whence can they grow, or whence derive increase,
Themselves the universe? or, if destroyed,
Where could they fly, from whom no space is void?
Thus still the same, though varied, equal still,
Each blent with each, the sphere of Being fill.

Ὡς δ' ὁπόταν γραφέες.—L. 83.

As when, an offering at some sacred shrine,
The skilful painters tint the rich design,

Upon the rainbow-pallet first they bruise,
Now more, now less, the harmonising hues.
Then every form its living likeness takes,
The grove, the flock, the human shape awakes;
The birds, the beasts, and those that swim the seas,
And the Immortal Gods, more great than these.
Thus all things born, and all that live below,
Forth from that elemental fountain flow.

Μορφὴν δ' ἀλλάξαντα.—L. 384.

THE son, but changed in form, the father slays.
Ah frantic sire! and as he strikes he prays.
No-tears avert the awful sacrifice,
He hears not; "On!" with maddening voice he cries,
And with dire banquet stains his shuddering hall.
Thus sires and mothers by their children fall,
Their kindred flesh the impious feast of all.

THE CAUSE AND CONSEQUENCE OF THE EXILE OF SOULS INTO THIS WORLD.

Ἔστιν Ἀνάγκης χρῆμα—L. 3.

THERE is a law of stern necessity,
And the great Gods confirmed the dread decree,
What spirit soe'er, of more than mortal strain,
With kindred blood his guilty limbs shall stain;
For ages must he roam this earth unblest,
Exiled, like me, from heaven, and here a pilgrim guest.

This thought is manifestly carried on in a passage in which the verse of Empedocles is buried in the prose of Plutarch. I endeavoured to unearth it.

Not from fair Greece the Lydian realms to change,
From Corinth to the Ægean isles to range;
But from the heavens, the moon's empyreal sphere,
O'er the sad fields of human life to err,
A banished outcast, still to pine and toil,
Like flowers that wither in a foreign soil.*

'Ηλύθομεν τόδ' ἐς ἄντρον.

For to this cave of gloom and sorrow come,
I wept and shrieked to see the unwonted home.

* * * *

Τὸν ἀτερπέα χῶρον.—L. 18.

The undelightful shore,
Where hosts of ill, where Carnage, Ire, and Hate,
Go darkly wandering o'er the fields of Fate.

THE GOLDEN AGE.

Οὐδέ τις ἦν κείνοισιν Ἄρης θεός.—L. 305.

Nor Mars was then a God, nor Tumult dire,
Nor monarch Jove, nor Jove's more ancient Sire;

---

* There are two lines which clearly belong to this passage :—
   Under the dire control of maddening strife.
And—
   From what a height of glory and of wealth.

Nor Neptune ruling on his watery throne.
Queen Aphrodite sate and reigned alone.
The only offerings on the blameless shrine,
The breathing stone, the painter's rich design.
And all sweet odours breathed and mingled there,
And purest myrrh and incense warmed the air;
Flowed liquid honey o'er the yellow floor,
The shrine stood guiltless of unhallowed gore;
Nor yet had flesh been slain, nor blood been spilt,
Nor man stood shuddering at the unheard-of guilt.

THE FATE OF THE WICKED.

Αἰθέριον μὲν γάρ σφε μένος.—L. 356.

These to the sea the indignant heavens shall cast;
The seas to earth repel, and earth in haste
Back to the unwearied sun and rolling heaven,
By each received, from each in hatred driven.

THE FATE OF THE BLESSED.

Εἰς δὲ τέλος.—L. 407.

But Bards, and Seers, and Leeches, first and best,
Here in their fellow-mortals' reverence blest,
To them at once expand the high abodes.
Heaven owns and welcomes the ascending Gods,
There at the immortal banquets still to be,
From human grief and fate for ever free.

ONOMACRITUS.

Grecian poetry had achieved all its glorious triumphs—its **Epics**, its Lyrics, and its Drama ; Greece itself, in its true greatness, had passed away, even before **the days of** Alexander. Yet the echoes of later Grecian poetry, even in the more artificial school of Alexandria, down to the better Byzantine epigrammatists of the Anthology, have riches of which most other countries might have been proud. In these echoes, I suspect, live some of the verses, only modernised, of the lost poets of the earlier and nobler period. Of the three great subjects of the old Greek heroic poetry—the Trojan war, the Thebaid, and the Argonautics —the last survives in **a few of the tragedies, and in what may be called the later, it may** be the feebler version, of Apollonius Rhodius. But in **Apollonius there** are lingering beauties which elsewhere would command high **admiration.** It cannot be forgotten how much the best parts of the Æneid owe to the Argonautics. There was an earlier poem on the subject, which bore the name of Orpheus, of course with no title to that all-hallowed and mysterious name.— It was perhaps by Onomacritus. From this poem I subjoin a passage.

Αὐτὰρ ἐμοὶ Μήδεια,—L. 952. Edit. Hermann.

ALOOF from all, save by my side alone,
Medea, on the awful verge and brink
Of the dire grove I stood. The triple trench
Deep in the level plain I dug, and there
Vast logs of juniper and cedar dry,
And crackling thorn and weeping poplar, heaped,
A hasty pyre sublime. Then many a drug
Forth from her caskets' fragrant sanctuary
Drew sage Medea. I beneath my robes

The waxen cakes slow kneaded; in the fire
Threw them; then sacrificed three chosen cubs
From the hounds' sable litter, with their blood
Mingling the marigold, the teasle tough,
The unfragrant fleabane, meadow saffron shred,
The red and choking bugloss. Filling thus
The victim's cauls, I placed them on the pyre.
The entrails, mixed with water, in the trench
I cast, then put my night-black raiment on,
Shook my dire steel, and prayed.
    They heard, they rose,
Bursting the void of the unlovely gulf,
Tisiphone, Alecto, and on high
Shaking their crackling torches' blood-red light,
Divine Megæra. Sudden flamed the trench,
The raging fires roared up; and vast outspread
A fog of ashes and foul smothering smoke.
Then all at once from Orcus through the fire
Pandora, Hecate, sprang up, and wheeled
Here and there round the awful trench; with them
Those Furies, dreadful, wondrous, merciless,
Eye may not gaze on them. An iron form
Was hers, by mortal men Pandora named;
And that three-headed multiform, a sight
Too dire to see, to comprehend too strange,
Hell's daughter, Hecate. A horse-head maned
From her left shoulder issued, from the right
A raging hound; her middle, shape had none;

And with both hands she swayed the two-edged sword.
Diana's guardian form let fall on earth,
Shuddering, her torch, and raised her eyes to heaven;
Fawned the dread watch-dogs; all the bolts sprang
    back
Of the dread cloister; burst the stately gates
All wide: the darksome grove stood all revealed.

APOLLONIUS RHODIUS.

We turn to the gentler pathos of Apollonius Rhodius in the Lamentation of Alcimede, his mother, at the departure of Jason.

Ὡς ἀδινὸν κλαίεσκεν.—Book i. l. 276. Edit. Brunck.

HER arms around her son the mother flung,
Still faster wept, and still more fondly clung;
So seeks the maid her aged nurse's breast,
Who, with no friend, no living kinsman blest,
Too long beneath a step-dame's cruel sway
Hath pined forlorn her weary life away;
Swells at her heart the big, the o'erpowering woe,
Nor choking words, and hardly tears will flow :
So weeping, clasping close that godlike man,
Her only son, Alcimede began—
  "Oh, on that dreadful day, when first I heard
King Peleus speak th' accurst, the fatal word,
Would I had died, my life, my sorrows done,
And thy dear hands had drest my bier, my son!
That only duty unfulfilled remains.
So fully hast thou paid thy mother's pains.
I of Achaia's dames most blest of all,
Most honoured; now, within my vacant hall,
Like some base slave, shall pine for thee, my boy!
Thee, once my pride, my glory, and my joy.

Thee first, and only thee, this bosom bore,
For stern Lucina loosed my zone no more.
O fate, that still impossible had seemed,
Even when my boding heart hath darkest dreamed."

THE LAUNCH OF THE ARGO.

τῶν ἐναμοιβαδὶς αὐτοί.—L. 380.

They on each side in silent order stand,
Spread the broad chest, and stretch the bony hand,
And Tiphys rose to give the signal word.
Soon as her loud and cheering shout they heard,
With one strong heave they lift from off its seat
The rooted bark. With swiftly following feet,
Down, down they urge her to the expectant tides,
And light and swift the Pelian Argo glides.
They on each side shout loud in emulous zeal,
Groan the strong planks beneath the rushing keel.
The smoking path with reek and dust is black,
Till on the sea she cleaves her foaming track,
Then with strong skilful arm they hold her steady back.

SHE SETS SAIL.

εἵλκετο δ' ἤδη πείσματα.—L. 533.

Now weighed the anchor, and the ship unmoored,
Upon the brine the red libation poured,
Jason alone his eyes, in silence, kept
Upon his native land, then turned away and wept.

The rest, as youths to Delphi's hallowed side,
Ortygia's shores, or blue Ismenus' tide,
In graceful dance, bright Phœbus' shrine around,
With steps harmonious beat the sacred ground;
So they to Orpheus' lyre accordant dashed
Their musical oars; the sparkling billows flashed,
And the dark brine was flecked with foaming light,
While roared the deep beneath the rowers' might;
The armour blazed against the golden sun,
The waters whitened in the vessel's run,
Like some broad pathway on a grassy plain,
Where bounds the bark along the yielding main.
From their bright shrines looked all Olympus down,
And Nymphs stood gazing on each mountain crown;
Much Pallas' mighty work admire, and more
Each hero bending o'er his pliant oar.
Came Chiron, prancing from the mountain's brow,
Round his moist hoofs the breaking waters flow;
To heaven he prayed, upraised his brawny hand,
Their safe return to bless their native land.
His wife held young Achilles up in joy,
And pointed out his sire to the proud boy.

AFTER MEDEA'S FIRST INTERVIEW WITH JASON.

αὔτως δ' αὖ Μήδεια.—iii. 451.

AND thus Medea slowly seemed to part,
Love's cares still brooding in her troubled heart;

And imaged still before her wondering eyes
His living, breathing self appears to rise—
His very garb; and thus he spake, thus sate,
Thus, ah, too soon! he glided from the gate.
Sure ne'er her living eyes beheld his peer,
And still his honied words are melting in her ear.

ἦ ῥα, καὶ ὀρθωθεῖσα.—B. iii. 645.

SHE said, she rose;
Her maiden chamber's solitary floor
With trembling steps she trod; she reached the door,
Fain to her sister's neighbouring bower to haste;
And yet the threshold hardly had she past,
Sudden her failing feet are checked by shame,
And long she lingered there, then back she came.
As oft desire would drive her forth again,
So oft does maiden bashfulness restrain.
Thrice she essayed to go, thrice stopped, then prone
In anguish on her couch behold her thrown.

MEDEA AT NIGHT.

νὺξ μὲν ἔπειτ' ἐπὶ γαῖαν.—L. 744.

'TWAS night, all earth in shadowy silence slept;
Lone on the deck his watch the sailor kept,
And gazed, where shines Orion's belt on high,
Or the Great Bear bestrides the northern sky.

The traveller couched beside his weary way;
Within his gate the drowsy warden lay.
Even by the couch, where lay her infant dead,
The mother drooped her sleep-o'erburthened head.
No bay of dogs disturbed the silent street,
Mute the dull hum, the tramp of moving feet.
'Twas darkness all, and voiceless silence deep;
Still from Medea fled the balmy-sleep.

Ἡ, καὶ φωριαμὸν μετεκίαθεν.—L. 802.

So she her fatal treasured casket sought,
With life and death in powerful compound fraught.
She placed it on her knees; the streams of woe
From her full eyes unchecked began to flow.
Long she bewailed her miserable state,
Then wildly seized the baleful drugs of fate.
Already hath she loosed the casket's band,
Sudden death's awful fear withholds her hand.
Then long she stood, to trembling doubt resigned,
And life's sweet cares came imaged to her mind.
She thought of all the joys of youth's glad years,
She thought of all her gentle maiden fears;
The very sun appeared to shine more bright,
As each fond image kindled on her sight.

THE FATAL INTERVIEW.

οὐδ' ἄρα Μηδείης θυμὸς τράπετ'.—L. 948.

Nor though she sing, will now her sweetest lay
With sweet diversion guile her cares away.
On any favourite air she dwelt not long,
Broke sudden off the faint unfinished song;
Nor on her train reposed her quiet gaze,
But restless down each distant pathway strays.
How burns her cheek, how bounds her heart to hear
The wind, or some light footstep trembling near.
Nor long delay—he burst upon her sight
Like Sirius from the ocean blazing bright,
That rises fair, but fatal to behold,
Darting red plagues upon the parching fold.
So Æson's lofty son arose to view,
As bright, as beauteous, but as dangerous too.
Then fell her heavy heart, her dim eyes swam,
O'er all her cheek the burning blushes came.
Nor fail her knees, her form nor onward bear,
But grown to earth, seem fixed and rooted there.
Slow glide the attendant maids away, while still,
Voiceless they gaze, and cannot gaze their fill.

CALLIMACHUS.

The Hymn, which in the Homeric days spoke in its freshness and with the mythology young and growing out of the creative belief, in Callimachus is become more stately and formal, but still not without force and grandeur. These Hymns were no doubt used in the public service. The following is the opening of that to Apollo :—

ʽΟΙΟΝ ὁ τἀπόλλωνος.—P. 6. Edit. Blomfield.

Lo! how Apollo's branching laurel shakes,
Lo! all at once the rocking temple quakes!
Lo! burst the doors! away, profane! away!
Himself with graceful step, the God of Day,
With sudden tremors bows the Delian palm:
Sweet sings the swan along the breathless calm.
Lift up, ye gates—unfold the dread abode;
Fall back, ye bolts—the God, behold the God!

The opening of the Elegy on the bathing of the statue of Minerva.

ʽΟΣΣΑΙ λωτροχόοι τᾶς Παλλάδος.—P. 47.

Come, wont to wait where in the secret shades
Great Pallas bathes, ye ministering maids!
The champing of the sacred steeds I hear;
Come, maids of Argos! Pallas' self is near.
The alabaster box of odours bring
(Sweet to the pipes the harmonious axles ring).
No perfumes rich, no costly ointments rare;
Unstained by these is Pallas' virgin hair;

Nor mirror bright her beauty's pride beseems,
That, changeless still, in conscious glory beams.
When judged the Phrygian boy that fatal strife
The mighty Goddess and Jove's awful wife
Disdained to gaze upon the burnished brass,
Disdained to gaze on Simois' liquid glass.
But by her mirror Venus stood, each hair
Once, twice, rebraiding with fastidious care.
The lofty Pallas, ere the strife began,
Twice the long stadium's measured circle ran.
Fleet and unbreathed, as by Eurotas' side,
Like shooting stars the youths of Sparta glide.
Then all her radiant form, anointed, gleams
With her own olive's pure and fragrant streams;
O'er all the face the mantling crimson glows,
Ye maids, like blushing peach, or opening rose.

ἔξιθ' Ἀθαναία περσέπτολι.—P. 49.

Come forth, destroyer of proud cities, come!
Come with thy golden casque and nodding plume;
Thou whom the crash of spear and shield delights,
Athene, come! the holy pomp invites.
Drink not to-day from the lone fountain's side,
Leave all unstained the river's hallowed tide.
In Physadea dip your urns to-day,
Or where cool Amymone's waters play.
Lo, Inachus, all rich with gold and flowers,
Forth from his mountain-springs redundant pours

A crystal bath for **heaven's** Immortal Maid.
O youths of Argos, shun **the** dangerous shade!
Who sees unveiled the Virgin Goddess chaste,
On Argos' beauteous towers has looked his last.

I add three Epitaphs from **Callimachus.**

τῇδε Σάων ὁ Δίκωνος ?—P. 56.

IN holy sleep here righteous Saon lies!
Say ye no more: the good man never dies.

Κρηθίδα τὴν πολύμυθον.—P. 58.

BLITHE Crethis, famed for many **a** sprightly **tale,**
With vain lament the Samian maids **bewail.**
Their pleasant, garrulous peer; in mute repose,
Who sleeps th' eternal sleep all nature **owes.**

τίς ξένος, ὦ ναυηγέ;—P. 68.

A **STRANGER!** who? A shipwrecked corpse unknown,
Leontichas entombed beneath this stone;
Mourning his own sad life, that finds no rest,
Like seabirds wandering **still** on ocean's breast.

LYCOPHRON.

I venture on two fragments out of the laboured mysteriousness of Lycophron, almost the only lines bordering on the intelligible. It was a strange effort to work up the pellucid clearness of Grecian poetry into a thick unnatural darkness.

'Ενὸς δὲ λώβης ἀντί.—L. 365. Edit. Reichard.

But for one dark offence all Hellas mourns
Her myriad sons' dark cenotaphs, not shrined
In golden urns, but on the sea-beat shore
Wide scattered; not with honoured ashes laid
Embalmed in their ancestral sepulchres.
But epitaphs o'er empty busts are wet
With scalding tears of mothers and of sons;
And those that filled of old one genial bed.

καὶ δὴ καταίθει γαῖαν.—L. 249.

Now Mars the reveller fires all the earth
With shouts, preluding to his lay of blood,
And all the blasted land lies waste and wide
Beneath us. Horrent gleam the fertile fields
With harvest thick of lances; in our ears
Rings from the lofty towers a startling cry,
High soaring to heaven's breathless mansions calm,
A cry of woman's grief, and garments rent:
" On horrors' head horrors accumulate."

s

THEOCRITUS.

With Theocritus we cannot think that we are still in learned and artificial Alexandria; indeed, but for the broad humour of the inimitable "Town Eclogue," the Praxinoe, we might suppose that we are reading a Sicilian, who never trod the streets of hot and dusty Alexandria, but had passed all his life in the pastoral plains or rich valleys of that fair island.

I have not done justice to Theocritus in these few lines.

*ἔν τε βαθείαις
ἁδείας σχίνοιο χαμευνίσιν ἐκλίνθημες.*
Idyllion, 7, 132. Edit. Gaisford.

On beds of fragrant mastic we recline,
And the fresh tendrils of the curling vine,
And many an ash and poplar overhead
Their cool and trembling canopy outspread.
Close by, the crystal fountain's holy wave
Flows gently murmuring from the Naiads' cave;
And in the leafy boughs, a summer sound,
The busy shrill cicala chirps around.
The nightingale sits warbling on the thorn,
The thrush and linnet pipe, the turtles mourn;
The yellow bees are flying to and fro
Where freshest flowers beside the fountain blow.
And all things breathe of summer's fertile hours,
And all things breathe of autumn's fruitage bowers.
Before our feet ripe golden fruits are strewn,
And vines beneath their purple load bow down.

ἅδιον, ὦ ποιμάν.—i. 7.

MORE sweet thy song than water's lulling flow
From some tall rock along the vale below.

ἀλλ' ἀφίκευ τὺ ποτ' ἄμμε.—xi. 42.

LEAVE the blue sea against its shores to rave,
And sweetly slumber in my noiseless cave;
The laurel there and cypress light are seen,
The vine and ivy blend their tenderest green;
There the cool rivulets that from Ætna's brow
The unfailing waters pour of liquid snow.

τυτθὸν δ' ὅσσον ἄπωθεν.—i. 45.

NOT far beyond that aged sea-worn man,
A vineyard, rich in purple wealth, began;
There sat a little boy the hedge beside,
Him with keen look two crafty foxes eyed.
One slowly stealing through the even rows,
Plundering the pendant fruit, in silence goes;
One to his wallet sidelong creeps, and sly,
And vows to leave him supperless and dry.
He careless at his pleasant labour set,
To catch the shrill cicala, weaves his net;
And smiling as he twines the pliant reeds,
Nor his rich charge nor rifled wallet heeds.

MOSCHUS.

αἲ αἲ ταὶ μαλάχαι.—iii. 106.

ALAS! the meanest herb that scents the gale,
The lowliest flower that blossoms in the vale,
Even where it dies, at spring's sweet call renews
To second life its odours and its hues.
But we, but man, the great, the brave, the wise,
When once in death he seals his failing eyes,
In the mute earth imprisoned, dark and deep,
Sleeps the long endless unawakening sleep.

τὰν ἅλα τὰν γλαυκάν.—v. 1.

WHEN gently skims the breeze the waters blue,
High swells my heart and kindles at the view;
The dull unmoving land delights no more,
The halcyon calm allures me from the shore.
But when the hoary deeps resound, the waves
Are hung with foam, and all the ocean raves,
Home to the land I look, and whispering trees,
And fly the smiling treachery of the seas.
Then the firm steadfast shore, the shadowy grove,
Where the pine sings in wildest winds, I love.
Oh, hard the fisher's life! the waves to reap;
His house his bark, his labours in the deep;
The wandering fish his miserable gain.
Mine the sweet sleep beneath the broad-leaved plane,
And mine the liquid fountain murmuring near,
That soothes, but ne'er disturbs the peasant's ear.

The poetry of Greece expires, not in its more inimitable form—the Epic (chanted by the rhapsodists in the palaces of the kings), or in the Lyric Poetry of the temple and the games, or the noble Drama. It has abdicated its higher functions; yet even in its dullest office—what we call **the** didactic—the ingenious and skilful versification of common **topics, there are gleams of felicitous language, of musical flow, which are worth hearing.**

ARATUS.

PROGNOSTICS OF A STORM.

Σῆμα δέ τοι ἀνέμοιο.—*Diosemeia*, i. 177. Edit. Matthiæ.

PRESAGE **the** storm, when swells **the breezeless deep**
O'er the flat sands and craggy headlands **steep**;
Rolls long and far a sullen booming sound,
The mountain-tops the **causeless** roar rebound.
When on the seaward breeze, with screaming cry,
O'er land the herons in dizzy circles fly;
**And, when the silent heavens are breathless, sail
The flocking gulls against the coming gale.
Oft the wild geese, and glancing divers stand,
With dripping pinions, on the sparkling sand.
The mist hangs lingering on the mountain's brow;**
And floating thistles' downs the winds foreshow,
When skimming o'er the silent deep they run,
And countless glitter in the gleaming sun;
　Expect ere long from thence fierce winds to rise,
Where sheeted lightnings fire the summer skies.

When frequent stars shoot through the sable night,
And trace their radiant path with glittering white,
Mark whence they fall, the storm is gathering there.
But when from diverse parts they cross and glare,
From every quarter dread the conflict dire
Of tempests raging in their furious ire.
When north and south, and east and west, the heaven
By the blue frequent lightning-shafts is riven,
Then fears the seaman on the dangerous main,
The heaving tides below, above the pouring rain.
And oft, the coming showers presaging, fly
Their fleecy clouds along the glittering sky,
Spanning the heaven the double bow appears,
And the stars darken in their halo'd spheres.
The birds that haunt the marsh, or ocean side,
Quick and unceasing plunge within the tide ;
Fast skim the swallows o'er the lucid lake,
And with their breasts the rippling waters break.
The wretched frogs, the sea-bird's fated prey,
Croak the long night their inharmonious lay ;
The lonely shrieking owl alarms the morn ;
The aged crow, on sable pinions borne,
Upon the beetling promontory stands,
And tells the advancing storm to trembling lands ;
Or dips and dives within the river's tide,
Or, croaking hoarse, wheels round in circles dark and wide.

THE GEOGRAPHY OF DIONYSIUS.

οὐ γάρ μοι βίος ἐστί.—L. 709. Edit. Matthiæ.

Not mine the merchant's life, o'er ocean dark
To launch my venturous patrimonial bark.
Ne'er voyage I from the Erythrean shore
To where old Ganges' fabled waters pour;
Nor mingle with the wild Hyrcanian clans, nor come
Where the red Avieni find their home
In the Caucasian glens of deepest gloom.
Me the wing'd Muses, through the yielding air,
O'er sea and land a toilless wanderer bear.
At home I sit, the unmeasured sea o'er-stray,
Mountains and plains, or soar through stars th' empyreal
  way.

THE SERES.

THE MANUFACTURE OF SILK.

καὶ ἔθνεα βάρβαρα Σηρῶν.—L. 752.

There the barbaric Serian tribes are born,
To feed the flocks, or herd the steer they scorn;
But weave the flowers their desert meadows yield,
And reap their costly robes from every field,
Soft as the spring-time verdure's smoothest leaves,
Thin as the finest web the spider weaves.

ARABIA.

πέζα δέ οἱ νοτίη.—L. 931.

Thence, southward bending to the Orient, laves
The Erythrean, with its ocean waves,
Of all earth's shores the fairest richest strand,
And noblest tribes possess that happy land.
First of all wonders, still for ever soar,
Sweet clouds of fragrance from that breathing shore.
The myrrh, the odorous cane, the cassia there,
And ever-ripening incense balms the air.
For in that land the all-ruling King on high
Set free young Bacchus from his close-bound thigh;
Broke odours from each tree at that fair birth,
And one unbounded fragrance filled the earth.
'Neath golden fleeces stooped th' o'er-laden flocks,
And streams came bounding from the living rocks.
Birds from strange isles, and many an untrod shore,
With leaves of cinnamon, were flying o'er.
Loose from his shoulders hung the fawn-skin down,
In his fair hair was wreathed the ivy-crown:
Ruddy his lips with wine. He shook his wand,
Smiling, and wealth o'erflowed the gifted land.
Whence still the fields with liquid incense teem,
The hills with gold, with odours every stream;
And in their pride her sumptuous sons enfold
Their limbs in soft attire and robes of gold.

THE PARTHIANS.

'Αλλ' ἤτοι πυλέων.—L. 1039.

There, the **Caspian** gates below,
The warrior **Parthians** bend the deadly bow;
Skilled in each art of war, they still disdain
To cleave with toilsome plough the fertile plain,
Nor with adventurous oar divide the deep,
Nor feed their flocks along the verdant steep.
From earliest youth the fatal bow they wield,
And mount the war-horse o'er the dusty field.
Still through the sounding land, of shaft and **lance**
Echoes the din, the trampling courser's prance.
They touch not food, save bathed from war's stern toil,
And all their banquet is their foeman's spoil.

OPPIAN.

COMPARISON OF THE HUNTER'S AND FISHERMAN'S LIFE.

χλούνην μὲν ὀρίτροφον.—*Halieutica,* i. 12. Edit. Schneider.

With sight distinct the hunter tracks his prey,
Wild swine or boar, beneath the eye of day.
Whether afar he hurl the fatal spear,
Or close in deadly conflict fierce and near,

On the firm earth the strife is waged. The hound
Tracks the wild game along the scented ground,
Even to his lair. Him many a calm retreat
From winter's frost and summer's parching heat
Awaits, where soft the breezy woodlands wave,
Or the cool rock o'erarches the still cave,
Where silver rivers from the mountain burst,
To bathe the limb, and slake the burning thirst;
And the soft meads their verdant couches spread
To rest at noon the smoothly-pillowed head.
And the wild woods their living fruits bestow,
And luscious feasts on every mountain glow,
No toil the hunter's life—one long delight.

*   *   *   *

Lurks the hard fishers' prey in depths unknown;
Hope flatters now, now like a dream is gone.
Not on the steadfast land they toil, but ride
Upon the bleak inconstant rolling tide:
Even from the shore, most awful to behold,
Where safe we stand, and yet the blood runs cold.
On slender planks, of every wind the slaves,
They wander, watching still the treacherous waves;
And ever shuddering at the empurpled seas,
Or billows darkening 'neath the rising breeze.
No shelter theirs from wind, or hail, or sleet,
Or the red dog-star's pestilential heat.

WHALE FISHING.

ἐσσυμένως δ' ἀκάτοισιν.—V. 154.

Swift in their boats along the noiseless tide,
Conversing in mute signs, they softly glide;
Beneath the quiet oars the whitening seas
Curl gently; not a sound is on the breeze,
Lest the huge whale be startled in his sleep,
And mock their toil, quick plunging in the deep.

τὸν δ' ὅτε παιφάσσοντα.—V. 227.

Now faint and panting lies the o'er-wearied whale,
Reels, drunk with pain; strength, wrath, and courage fail,
And adverse fate inclines her sinking scale.
The fisher watches with exulting eyes
The bladder, harbinger of victory, rise.
Lightly it dances o'er the brine afar.
As, after some wide-wasting deadly war,
Around the white-robed herald crowds the throng,
Welcoming the news of peace with shout and song;
Even with such joy they see the skins emerge;
Another and another skims the surge,
Dragging the mighty monster, yet alive,
Reluctant, but too feeble now to strive.
High swells the fisher's heart, with rapid oars,
Around their prey their little navy pours.
Now dash the waves, and wild the din and wide,
Of shout and clamorous voices o'er the tide.

Ye might have thought some furious battle raged,
And man with man the deathful contest waged.
Afar the herdsman on the sea-beat rock,
Or shepherd, as he feeds his mountain flock,
Or woodsman, stooping at his noon-day toil,
Or hunter, as he tracks his flying spoil,
Starts at the sound, and on the beetling brow
Of some tall promontory peers below,
To see the issue of this contest dread,
And the wild war o'er all the ocean spread.

The following tale is also told—in some points better told—in Ælian, *De Nat. Animal.*

'Αλλ' οὐδ' ἠϊθέοιο πόθους.—V. 458.

STILL on the Æolian shore the tale is sung,
No ancient tale, but still in living memory young,
The island boy how once the dolphin loved,
Nor ever from those hallowed waters roved,
But dwelt a denizen of that smooth bay,
Basked on its waves, or in its cool depths lay.
Of youths, the fairest he, the island's grace:
The fish, the swiftest of the watery race,
 Day after day, along the crowded shore,
Still would the island's wondering thousands pour,
Light to his boat the boy would spring alone,
Call the familiar name, to both well known,
The name from childhood's earliest hours endeared.
Swift as an arrow, when that sound he heard,

The silver dolphin gleamed beneath the deck,
Fawned with his tail, and curled his glittering neck;
Fain would he touch the boy, with motion bland
Who smoothed him down, and soft caressing hand.
Then leaped the boy within the yielding tide,
And lo! the loving dolphin by his side;
And cheek to cheek, and side to side, he prest,
And curled, and glanced, and wantoned round his breast;
He seemed as he would fondly kiss his face,
Or gently fold him in his cool embrace.
Soon as the shore they neared, the youth bestrode
His scaly back, and there in triumph rode.
Still where would guide the blithe and sportive boy,
The obedient fish went bounding in its joy;
Now where the deeper billows heave and roar,
Now smoothly glide along the quiet shore.
Nor e'er might skilful charioteer command
A steed more docile to his mastering hand,
Nor at the hunter's beck the well-trained hound
Track the fleet prey, and scent the tainted ground,
As this unbridled dolphin would obey
His self-chosen master's light and easy sway;
Nor him alone, all toil at his behest
Was pleasure, him to serve was to be blest.
So each in turn his blithe companions rode,
And light the dolphin bore th' unwonted load,
Such all his life the faithful love he bore.
    But the youth died—then all along the shore

Was sadly seen the mourning fish to roam;
At first seemed wondering that he did not come,
And searched each nook, each creviced rock in vain,
Ye almost heard a feeble voice complain.
Nought heeded he the crowds along the sands,
Nor took the offered food from strangers' hands;
Then far he fled to the great deep, nor more
Was seen to haunt that solitary shore,
Nor long survived his dear, his human mate,
But shared his living sports, and shared his fate.

NICANDER.

THE ASP,

so-called. In some respects this serpent more resembles the boa, but its bite is venomous.

Φράζεο δ' αὐαλέαις.—*Ther.* L. 157. Edit. Bandini.

Now horrent all with rigid scales describe
The murtherous asp, most sluggish of its tribe.
On its strait path it glides with impulse strong,
And drags its vast unwinding bulk along,
A fearful form! in heavy sloth it lies,
For ever winking with its sleepy eyes;
Yet, hear it but a sound, a voice—behold,
Off falls the sleep, unwinds each spiry fold,
Distended wide the mighty coil appears,
And high and fierce the quivering head uprears.

Six feet in length its earth-born bulk expands,
Its thickness, as a lance by craftsman's hands
Hewn from the ash, to meet in daring fight,
The mountain bull, the roaring lion's might.
The hue that runs along its dusky back
Paler and spotted now, now ashy black;
Or like the sable Ethiopian soil,
Where meets the sea the many-mouthèd Nile.
Two horn-like wens protrude upon the brows;
Beneath the blood-red eye, deep-sunken glows.
But should the hapless traveller cross its path,
Full swells the ashen neck with bursting wrath.
Four venomous teeth are rooted in its jaws,
Crooked and long, the covering film withdraws,
When from its secret cell the poison flows;
O may such awful death befall my foes!
Smooth and unwounded seems the ruddy skin,
Nor, painless, swells without, nor burns within:
O'er all th' unstruggling man death seems to creep,
And down he sinks to everlasting sleep.

DEATH FROM OPIUM.

καὶ σὺ δὲ μήκωνος.—Alex. 433.

Now hear how softly soothe to fatal sleep
The liquid tears the dropping poppies weep.
The limbs, in all their pale extremities,
Turn deathly cold; the dull scarce-opening eyes

Beneath their heavy lids unmoving glow :
Through every pore unfragrant moistures flow ;
Wan all the face, the lips all fire within ;
Loose, and disjointed, hangs the dropping chin ;
Slow, and unfrequent comes the struggling breath
Through the parch'd throat ; and of approaching death
The livid nails th' unthinking wretch apprize,
Dilated nostrils, and deep-sunken eyes.

ANTHOLOGIA.

The edition referred to is the Anthologia **Palatina—Jacobs.**

MELEAGER.

αἰεί μοι δινεῖ.—i. p. 145.

STILL Love's sweet voice is trembling in mine ears,
Still silent flow mine eyes with Love's sweet tears;
Nor night nor day I rest; by magic spells
Stamped on my soul the well-known image dwells.
O Love! how swift thy flight to reach the heart,
Thy wings are only powerless to depart.

ἀνθοδίαιτε μέλισσα.—P. 129.

O FLOWER-FED bee, for Heliodora's cheek,
  Why thus forsake the dewy cups of spring?
Of love, a graceful emblem, wouldst thou speak,
  Its honey sweets, its keen and bitter sting?
Yes, thou repliest—Away! what thou wouldst tell,
The lover's monitress, we know too well.

RUFINUS.

πέμπω σοι Ῥοδόκλεια.—P. 105.

With mine own hands of choicest flowers I wove
A chaplet, Rodoclea, for my love.
The lily there and blushing rose are met,
Narcissus moist and blue-eyed violet.
Gaze on their leaves, and cease from pride, fair maid,
Thou and those flowers alike must bloom and fade.

AGATHIAS.

τί στενάχεις; φιλέω.—P. 165.

' Thou sigh'st?" " for love." " Of whom?" " a maid."
    " Most fair?"
" Fair to mine eyes and sweet beyond compare."
" When, where didst thou behold her?" " At a feast,
Reclining on a couch, a graceful guest."
" Dost fly the lawful marriage-bond? Too sure,
Alas! I know her dowerless state: she's poor."
" Thou know'st, then lov'st thou not; 'tis all untrue:
For who can love and soundly reason too?"

Ἦ ῥά γε καὶ σύ, Φίλιννα.—P. 171.

Thou, too, Love's pains, Philinna, dost thou bear,
    And sit and pine away with tearless eye?
Or of my griefs nor taking thought nor care,
    In sweet unbroken slumber dost thou lie?

Thy time will come, and I shall see the streams
   Of tears, relentless! that smooth cheek o'ercloud;
For Venus with one virtue still redeems
   Her countless cruelties—she hates the proud.

MELEAGER.

SPRING.

χείματος ἠνεμόεντος.—ii. 125.

DARK winter's storms are o'er; the heavens smile bright
With flowery-mantled Spring's empurpling light,
The earth its robe of palest green assumes,
And every plant with youthful flowerets blooms.
Still as Aurora's nectar-dews they quaff,
With opening roses gay the meadows laugh;
The shepherd pipes along the mountain steep,
The snowy flocks around the goat-herd leap;
The mariner to Zephyr's blandest gale
Spreads o'er the ocean his embosom'd sail.
With richest promise to the God of wine,
The trailing vines their flowering tendrils twine.
The yellow bee at its sweet labour dwells,
And broods and murmurs in its waxen cells.
And everywhere the glad birds wake the song:
The halcyon skimming the blue waves along,
The swallow twittering from her roof-built nest,
The swan that spans the wave with mantling breast;
The nightingale, the grove's melodious guest.

If blooming flowers are glad, and earth is bright,
And sings the swan, and flocks are bounding light,
And seamen sail, and Bacchus leads the glee,
Carols the bird, and hums the toiling bee;
How may the Poet's heart alone be mute,
And mock the joyous Spring with silent lute?

THE CICALA TO THE PEASANT.

(Unknown.)

τίπτ' ἐμὲ τὸν φιλέρημον.—ii. 130.

O tear not thus, relentless swains, your prey,
The lone Cicala from her dewy spray,
The Dryads' wayside nightingale, whose tune
Soothes hills and groves beneath the burning noon.
Uninjured, lo, the thrush, the blackbird feeds,
And many a sparrow thieves the scattered seeds.
Go, the wing'd plunderers of the field pursue,
But grudge not me my leaves and liquid dew.

NICIAS.

Αἰόλον ἱμεροθαλὲς ἔαρ.—ii. 200.

Thou glancing bee, sweet herald of the spring,
Lover of earliest flowers, thy yellow wing
Light on some fragrant spot, and ply thy toil,
And fill thy waxen chambers with the spoil.

ÆSOPUS.

πῶς τις ἄνευ θανάτου.—ii. 315.

O how to 'scape thee without Death, sad Life!
'Tis hard to fly, more hard to bear the strife.
How beautiful all nature, earth, and ocean;
The stars, the moon, the sun's majestic motion!
Sorrow and fear the rest, an instant brief
Of joy, the next the sure avenging grief.

PALLADAS.

προσδοκίη θανάτου.—ii. 298.

The dread of death is one eternal pain,
At least from this, release by death we gain;
Weep not for him who breathes his parting breath—
There is no second suffering after death.

LOCAL INSCRIPTIONS.

THE FOUNTAIN.

Νύμφαι Ἀμαδρυάδες.—i. 245.

NYMPHS of the fount, who in this cool retreat
Walk the clear waters with your rosy feet,
Hail and preserve Cleonymus, your shrines
Who placed beneath the tall and whispering pines.

A STATUE OF PAN PIPING.

σιγάτω λάσιον.—ii. 276.

YE waving woods, be silent on the hill!
Ye dripping founts and lowing herds, be still!
Hark, Pan himself, to wake the liquid song,
Runs, with moist lip, the vocal reeds along;
While round, in graceful dance, harmonious move
The Nymphs that haunt the fountain and the grove.

ANTIPATER.

A PLANE OVERGROWN BY A VINE.

αὔην με πλατάνιστον.—ii. 78.

O'ER my dry trunk this gentle vine hath grown,
And hung my boughs with verdure not their own.

The plane that, when her young shoots blossomed first,
'Mid my broad leaves her purple clusters nursed.
So choose the mistress of thy heart, whose faith
Clings, and repays thy fondness even in death.

A STATUE OF PAN NEAR A FOUNTAIN.

"Ερχεο καὶ κατ' ἐμάν.—ii. 628.

COME sit beneath my pine, whose whispering top
   Sounds, gently bending to the breathing west:
Lo, where the falling waters slowly drop,
   I sing and soothe the lonely reeds to rest.

THE TRAVELLER.

τᾷδε κατὰ χλοεροῖο.—ii. 694.

HERE, traveller, on the verdant mead at ease,
   Repose thy weary limbs all careless thrown;
Here the pine whispers to the gentle breeze,
   The sweet cicala chants her soothing tone;
And here the shepherd haunts the fountain stream,
   And sits and pipes beneath the broad-leaved plane,
Flying the autumnal Dog-star's fatal beam.
   To-morrow to the weary road again!

VOTIVE INSCRIPTIONS.

These are of all classes—I suspect of all ages: the votive offerings of the arms of the warrior and the lyre of the poet, the net of the fisherman and the shuttle of the weaver. It is a curious feature of Greek life and religion.

SIMONIDES.

THE ARMS OF THE WARRIOR.

[τόξα τάδε πτολέμοιο.—i. 185.

HERE, ceasing from their warlike toil, our bows
Beneath Athene's guardian roof repose;
Oft, 'mid the manly strife and battle-cry,
Bathed in the blood of Persia's chivalry.

MNASALCAS.

σοὶ μὲν καμπύλα τόξα.—i. 187.

PHŒBUS! here I hang for ever
Bow unstrung and shaftless quiver.
Ask ye where our winged darts?
Seek them in our foemen's hearts.

ANYTA.

ἔσταθι τῇδε κράνεια.—i. 227.

So stand thou there, my murtherous lance, no more
Thy brazen talons drip with hostile gore:
But in Athene's high and marble dome
Proclaim the Cretan's might in years to come.

MACEDONIUS.

THE POET'S LYRE.

Τὴν κιθάρην Εὔμολπος.—i. 213.

BLAMING his aged hands' expiring fire,
Eumolpus placed on Phœbus' shrine his lyre,
And said, "Be mute, my harp; no more I try
To wake thy old forgotten harmony;
Leave the sweet strings to youth's ecstatic touch,
While my cold hands cling trembling to their crutch."

THE SHEPHERD'S CROOK.

Δάφνις ὁ συρικτάς.—i. 210.

DAPHNIS, whose pipe the listening herdsman cheers,
Now bowed my trembling hand with weight of years.
To Pan, the shepherd's God, my crook I bear,
And bid adieu to all my pastoral care.
Yet still my pipe shall sound; my limbs may fail,
My voice, unfainting, chants its jocund tale.

Yet to the wolves, that on the mountain rage,
Tell not the tidings of my useless age.

THE DRUNKARD TO HIS CASK.

Οἰνοπότας Ξενοφῶν.—i. 211.

BACCHUS! take my empty cask,
'Tis all I have, all thou canst ask.

THE FISHER'S NET.

ταῖς Νύμφαις Κινύρης.—i. 193.

TAKE ye my net, ye Nymphs, my strength is past,
Nor may this arm its spreading circles cast.
Now sport, ye fish, in fearless pastime free;
My age gives peace to all the silent sea.

ANTIPATER.

THE MAIDEN'S DISTAFF.

κερκίδα τὰν ὀρθρινά.—i. 236.

THE shuttle heard, ere twittered on the roof
The earliest swallow, halcyon of the woof;
The distaff nodding with its rattling sound,
The thread that ran the rapid wheel around,
The web, the faithful basket ever full
With the smooth flax and fleecy well-combed wool—
Young Telesilla offers on the shrine
Of the industrious Maiden Queen divine.

PHANIUS.

THE SCHOOLMASTER'S OFFERING.

Σκήπωνα προποδαγόν.—i. 283.

The staff that propped my feet, the strap, the cane,
The well-known terror of the youthful train;
The ring to which the culprits hung, one shoe,
The nightcap to my bald head ever true—
To Hermes these, the insignia of his rule,
Old Callon gives, and abdicates his school.

AGATHIAS.

THE MARINER'S OFFERING TO THE HAVEN GOD.

Εὔδια μὲν πόντος.—i. 284.

Smooth lies the surface of the purple seas,
Nor curled nor whitened by the gentle breeze.
No more, hoarse dashing from the breakers steep,
The heavy waves recoil into the deep.
The zephyrs breathe, the murmuring swallow weaves
Her straw-built chamber 'neath the shadowy eaves.
Fear not, bold mariner, the Syrtes sand,
Nor Sicily's inhospitable strand,
If first before the haven God you burn
The votive offering for your safe return.

DEDICATORY.

BACCHYLIDES.

TO THE ZEPHYR.

Εὔδημος τὸν νηόν.—L. 202.

To Zephyr, gentlest wind that fans the air,
   Eudemus dedicates this lowly fane,
Who, instant as he poured the votive prayer,
   Came winnowing from its husk the golden grain.

A BRAZEN FROG.

τὸν Νυμφῶν θεράποντα.—L. 199.

Slave of the Nymphs, the songster of the pool,
The frog that haunts the waters clear and cool;
The traveller, rescued from the deadly drought,
Here imaged in the votive brass, has brought.
As in his burning way he toiled along,
Came from her dewy cell the welcome song;
And he, obedient to her guiding voice,
Found the glad stream that made his heart rejoice.

THE CICALA.

τὸν χαλκοῦν τέττιγα.—i. 202.

PHŒBUS, on thy shrine I place
Thine own Cicala wrought in brass,
Memorial of my victor crown,
Eunomus of Locri's town!
To the lyre's sweet strife we came
(Parthes was my rival's name).
To the plectrum's touch of fire
Scarce had rung the Locrian lyre;
With the sharp and sudden strain
Burst the shrilling string in twain.
Ere the halting harmony
On the list'ning ear could die,
Sat the insect, carolling
Sweetly on the broken string,
To the same unfailing note,
Warbling from his mimic throat.
She whose song of old beguiled
Only woodland echoes wild;
Sung in perfect unison,
To the harp's unwonted tone.
Hence, Latona's son divine,
Votive on thy holy shrine,
From my glad and grateful hands,
The little brazen minstrel stands.

INSCRIPTIONS RELATING TO THE FINE ARTS.

This cluster of Epigrams seems to me singularly interesting as illustrative of ancient art, and showing the estimation in which certain works were held.

THE JOVE OF PHIDIAS.

ἦ Θεὸς ἦλθ' ἐπὶ γῆν.—ii. 647.

STOOPED Jove, O Phidias, from his bless'd abode?
Or soar'd thy soul to see the awful God?

THE BACCHANAL OF SCOPAS.

ἔκφρονα τὴν Βάκχην.—ii. 641.

THE Bacchanal who maddened? Art alone,
Not Nature, mingling phrenzy with the stone.

THE HERCULES OF POLYCLETUS.

χαλκὸν ἀποιμώζοντα.—ii. 653.

WHO taught the brass to groan? Whose plastic mind,
Such strength, such effort, in one form combined?
A living work! Th' Herculean toil and might
I see, and weep and shudder at the sight.
See, lifted in his arms, Antæus gasp,
And writhing, seem to shriek within his grasp.

THE BULL OF MYRO.

Βουκόλε, τὰν ἀγέλαν.—ii. 248.

GRAZE, swain, thy herd afar, nor with thee drive
Fam'd Myro's brazen bull, as if alive.

Βοῦν ἰδίαν.—ii. 249.

AMIDST a herd his heifer Myro sought,
Drove off the rest, and then his own he caught.

THE ALEXANDER OF LYSIPPUS.

Λύσιππε πλάστα.—ii. 661.

WHAT living fire, Lysippus, bright and warm,
Breathes in great Alexander's brazen form?
Who now shall blame the Persians' dastard flight?
The herds will ever fly the lion's might.

THE HERCULES DESPOILED OF HIS ARMS, BY LYSIPPUS.

Ἡράκλες ποῦ σοι.—ii. 655.

WHERE thy rough club, O Hercules? where now
Thy Nemean lion's skin? thy fatal bow?
Thy strength and sternness where? now gentle grown,
How hath Lysippus tamed the tranquil stone?
Who thus the unconquered Hero dared despoil?
'Twas Love, his one insuperable toil.

THE CNIDIAN VENUS OF PRAXITELES.

τίς λίθον ἐψύχωσε.—ii. 674.

WHO saw bright Venus, radiant from above?
And kindled all the stone, instinct with love?
Praxiteles. Her Queen Olympus mourns,
Who from her Cnidian fane no more returns.

THE ATHENIAN PALLAS.

τὰν Κνιδίαν Κυθέρειαν.—ii. 677.

STRANGER, the Cnidian Venus hast thou seen?
Thou say'st, Lo, Gods and men, your rightful Queen?
Gaze on Athenian Pallas' awful brow!
Thou criest, O Paris, what a clown wert thou!

THE SATYR OF PRAXITELES.

τέχνας εἵνεκα σεῖο.—ii. 256.

WHAT art hath bound me here in lifeless trance?
Off, set me free, and let me join the dance!
Think not the Satyr joyless grown and old!
The envious marble will not lose its hold.

LEONIDAS.

THE ANACREON OF XANTHIPPUS.

ἴδ' ὡς ὁ πρέσβυς.—ii. 719.

LOOK how, on his drunken heel,
Old Anacreon seems to reel.

Round his feet his robe hangs down,
One shoe lost and one shoe on.
Still of love he seems to sing,
Still to strike the breathing string.
Hold him, Bacchus, hold him fast,
Hold him, or he'll fall at last!

THE VENUS OF APELLES.

τὰν ἀναδυομέναν.—ii. 679.

BEHOLD the triumph of Apelles' art,
Fair Venus from her mother Ocean start.
Her hand enwreathing in her hair, she presses
The dewy foam from her loose falling tresses.
Humbled, Minerva's self and Juno bow:
"In beauty's strife we dare not meet thee now."

THE SAME.

ἀλλὰ τάχος.—ii. 680.

RASH gazer, from the canvas pass away,
Or the prest hair will wet thee with its spray.

ANTIPHILAS.

THE MEDEA OF TIMOMACHUS.

τὰν ὀλοὰν Μήδειαν.—ii. 667.

TIMOMACHUS, thy fell Medea strove
At once with jealous wrath and mother's love.

A wondrous work, two passions to combine,
Fierce ire and pity, in one rich design.
Yet perfect both, her menace melts to tears,
And, through her beauty bursting wrath appears.
Yet pause! pursue the awful tale no more,
And shrink repugnant from the infant's gore.

From the Poem descriptive of the statues in the Gymnasium at Constantinople. The first, Deiphobus, singularly resembles the statue usually called the Fighting Gladiator in the Louvre, except the helmet.

Δηίφοβος μὲν πρῶτος.—*Anthologia*, Jacobs, iii. p. 161.

First, on his high-wrought pedestal, behold,
With helmed head, Deiphobus the bold,
Such as before his falling palace gate,
Stern Menelaus' onset to await,
He stood; advancing as in act to strike,
Yet to one side he seem'd to turn oblique,
And drawing up his arching back, his might
Gathered for one dread blow. Yet still his sight,
As of some foe's dark onset well aware,
Wandering around, on all sides seemed to glare.
His left hand forward holds his ample shield,
High raised the right, the glittering sword to wield.
Already that stern hand had struck the foe,
But the hard brass restrains the deadly blow.

HECUBA.

The statue, now, I believe, called the Præfica, was once thought to be Hecuba.

τίς σε πολυτλήμων Ἑκάβη.—ibid. 176.

WHAT more than mortal skill hath taught to glow,
O wretched Hecuba! thy voiceless woe?
Lives in the brass thy unextinguished grief,
Nor pitying art hath given thy pains relief.
There in thine agony stand'st thou; now no more
Seem'st thou the valiant Hector to deplore,
Nor sad Andromache's disastrous fate,
But the dire fall of Troy's imperial state.
Drawn o'er thy face the robe thy anguish shows,
And the loose veil that to thy sandals flows.
Thy soul is struggling with grief's last extreme,
Upon thy cheeks the gushing tears would stream;
But quenched the moist and liquid tide appears,
The drought of grief has parch'd up all thy tears.

EPITAPHIA.

I have given before one or two examples of the exquisite simplicity of the Greek monumental inscriptions. Sometimes, indeed, but how rarely has Christian hope expressed itself with the same quiet beauty!

PHILETAS.

ἀ στάλα βαρύθουσα.—i. 453.

THIS mourning column tells, that early death,
Theodota, hath stopped thy infant breath.
The infant to her grieving sire replies:
"He 'scapes the ills of life who earliest dies."

LEONIDAS OF TARENTUM.

Αὐτὰ ἐπὶ Κρήθωνος.—i. 532.

Lo, Crethon's monument, his name survey;
Beneath is Crethon's self, but turned to clay.
Once was his wealth, O Gyges, vast as thine;
And countless flocks were his, and countless kine.
Once was—what more? the envy of his race!
And now of earth he fills no wider space.

ἠχήεσσα θάλασσα.—i. 505.

O SOUNDING sea, why thus with tempests dark
Hast thou o'erwhelmed that unpresuming bark,

And underneath thy drowning waters thrown
Young Teleutagoras, Timarion's son?
O'er his pale corpse, upon some desert shore,
The funeral wail the gulls and seamews pour;
While old Timarion, by an empty tomb,
Weeps Teleutagoras' untimely doom.

Ἆ δειλ' Ἀντίκλεις.—i. 447.

ALAS for Anticles! alas for me
My one sweet child upon his bier to see.
Ere eighteen years were o'er, my child, thou'rt gone!
I sit and weep in orphan'd age alone.
Were I in Death's dark house! The dawn of day
Delights not me, nor Phœbus' golden ray.
Mightst thou not end, dear Anticles! the strife,
Bearing me with thee from this wretched life.

DIOTIMUS.

Αὐτόμαται δειλαί.—i. 355.

AT eve the silent steers were seen to come,
Beat with the pelting snow, spontaneous home.
Alas! Timomachus, beside the oak,
Lies smitten by the fatal lightning-stroke.

DIOSCORIDES.

Εἰς δηίων πέμψασα.

Demœnete sent forth, at war's stern call,
Eight sons, and in one tomb she buried all.
She shed no tear, she said but this, no more:
"Sparta! for thee alone my sons I bore."

DAMAGETUS.

πρὸς σὲ Διός.—i. 471.

Stranger! by hospitable Jove we pray,
Thus in old Thebes to sad Charinus say,
That Menis here and Polynices sleep;
And add—their early doom they do not weep,
Though fallen by Thracian arms; they only grieve
Their sire in destitute old age to leave.

ἡ πυρὶ πάντα τεκοῦσα.—ii. 87.

I that bore children only for the pyre,
Philinna, saw three sons within the fire.
I took a stranger offspring to my care,
For those I hoped might live I did not bear,
And beautiful grew up th' adopted boy;
But envious heaven denied the borrowed joy:
It took my fatal name, and died—who's she
E'er bore a child, who sorrows not for me?

HYMNS.

I subjoin two fragments here, of a late period probably, which have been first published in the *Philosophoumena* of Hippolytus, **bishop of Porto, published as the work of Origen.** The translation follows the restoration of Schneidewin. It illustrates the spirit of its strange mysticism, the worship **of Cybele, Atys, or some native god or goddess,** or both.

Εἴτε Κρόνου γένος.—P. 118.

Son of Saturn! son of Jove!
Or born of mighty Rhea's love.
Holy name that sounds so dear
To that ancient Rhea's ear!
Thee the old Assyrians all
The thrice-wept Adonis call.
To thee for name hath Egypt given,
The holy horned moon of heaven!
Thou the serpent-god of Greece!
The all-reverenced Adam thou of Samothrace!

Thee the Lydians, Phrygians thee,
Invoke, the Corybantic deity:
Thee Pappus now, and now the dead,
Now lifting up, reborn, the godlike head;
Unfruitful now on barren desert brown,
Now the rich golden harvest mowing down;
Or whom the blossoming almond-tree
Brought forth on the free hills a piper blithe to be.

*   *   *

Atys, old Rhea's son, I sing,
Not with the wild bells' clashing ring;
Nor Ida's fife, in whose shrill noise
The old Kouretæ still rejoice;
But with the mingling descant meet
Of Phœbus' harp, so soft, so sweet.
Evan! Evan! Pan, I call
Evan! the wild Bacchanal;
Or that bright shepherd that on high
Folds the white stars up in the silent sky.

TO HECATE.

MAGICAL INCANTATION FROM THE SAME.

Νερτερίη, χθονίη τε.

TRIPLE Goddess, Bombo! come!
Of earth, and heaven, and nether gloom!
By the wayside thine the seat;
And wheresoe'er three highways meet!
Bearer thou of flashing light;
Walking in the depths of night;
Hater of the sun's glad power,
Comrade of the darksome hour;
Rejoicing in the savage howl,
And the blood of bandogs foul!
Thou upon the dead that walkest;
O'er the dismal barrows stalkest;

For the blood-libation red
Athirst, sad mortals' direst dread !
Gorgo, Mormo, and the Moon !
Come, propitious come, and soon !
Thousand-formed ; arise ! arise !
And share our solemn sacrifice !

QUINTUS CALABER.

I cannot but think, that in these late poets of the Trojan war, survive, modernised perhaps and harmonised to the ear of an unheroic race, many fragments of the old posthomeric poetry: that vast cycle which, wanting the unity of the Iliad and of the Odyssey, yet were current and popular in the songs of the other rhapsodists. These furnished, like Homer himself, much of their rich materials to the tragedians, and even to Virgil and Ovid. I am persuaded that the late revival of the Trojan legends in Quintus Calaber, Tryphiodorus, Coluthus, was rather a *rifacciamento* than original.

THETIS AND AURORA BEHOLDING THE COMBAT OF MEMNON AND ACHILLES.

'Αμφὶ Θέτιν Νηρῆος.—ii. 497. Edit. de Pau.

ROUND Thetis stood
The anxious daughters of the hoary flood;
Trembled the great Achilles' fate to hear,
While each immortal cheek grew pale with fear.
Nor less for Memnon feared the bright-haired Morn,
In her swift car through trackless ether borne.
Around their Queen, in motionless amaze,
The daughters of the Sun admiring gaze,
Through that wide circle where the gold-haired God
By Jove's command pursues his yearly road.

THE PARTING OF NEOPTOLEMOS FROM HIS MOTHER DEIDAMIA.

ὃς δ'ἐρατεινὸν
Μειδιόων.—vii. 312.

A BEAUTEOUS smile upon his brow,
Swift to the ships the youth essayed to go.
Yet still his mother's tearful converse sweet
Within their home delayed his hurrying feet.
The seated rider so his noble horse
Restrains—all fire and panting for the course:
With quick impatient neigh he champs the bit,
And his broad chest with flakes of foam is wet;
Still paw his restless feet the echoing ground,
And loud and far is heard the trampling sound;
The chestnut mane is loosely floating wide,
And all the rider's heart dilates with pride.
So, as she held him, still with lofty joy
Gazed the proud mother on her parting boy.

  * * * *

A thousand times he kissed her, then was gone;
She in her father's palace stood alone.
As underneath some mansion's marble eaves,
Her many-coloured young the swallow grieves.
On them the crafty snake hath made his feast.
She flutters now around her plundered nest;
Now down the lofty colonnade she flies,
And feebly chirps her melancholy cries.

So her lost son Deidamia wept,
Still on the bed, where he once softly slept;
Or stood in tears beside the door, or prest
And fondly treasured in her lonely breast
Some idle plaything to his childhood dear;
Or haply slumbering on the wall, a spear,
Or ought his hand had hallowed with its touch,
She could not kiss too oft, or love too much.
He, heedless all the while, and hurrying far,
Shot to the fleet, like some swift-flying star.

ULYSSES AND NEOPTOLEMOS APPROACHING AND IN VIEW OF THE SHORES OF TROY.

τοῖσι δ' ἄρ' Ἰδαίων.—vii. 400.

As rose in heaven the morning clear and bright,
Ida's long towery ridge appeared in sight;
Next Chrysa's isle, and Smintheus' holy fane,
Then bold Sigeum beetling o'er the main;
And great Pelides' tomb—that point alone
With gentle care Ulysses to the Son
Delayed, far rising o'er the waves, to show,
Cautious to wake the deep but slumbering woe.

THE TROJAN YOUTH GOING FORTH TO BATTLE.

Καναχὴ δὲ κατὰ πτόλιν.—ix. 111.

The brazen din through all the city pealed,
Of youth all arming for the bloody field.

Here clung the wife, yet shrunk, and wept to feel,
Supplanting her embrace, the hard cold steel;
And infants here, with o'er-officious care,
Essay their sires' unwieldy arms to bear.
He wept awhile in anguish, then in joy
And pride stood gazing on the playful boy.
In his full heart the brave resolve grew high,
For them to conquer, or for them to die.
Here busy by his son the old man stands,
Fits all his armour with experienced hands;
And much exhorts him basely ne'er to yield,
But bear him bravely in the fatal field;
On his own aged breast displays the scars,
The deep and glorious signs of ancient wars.

APOLLO APPEARS IN DEFENCE OF THE TROJANS.

καὶ τότε δὴ Τρώεσσιν.—ix. 291.

Troy fled; but instant at the sight
Sprang forth, all fury, from Olympus' height
Latona's son. Clouds wrapt his awful form,
As down he rode upon the volleying storm.
Irradiate in his golden arms he came,
Burned his bright path, as with the lightning's flame.
Behind him, as he went, his quiver rang,
Pealed the vast air, earth echoed back the clang.
With feet unweary Xanthus' shore he trod:
One loud and dreadful shout proclaimed the God.

THE DEATH OF PARIS.

He is at the feet of Œnone.   'Αλλ' ἄγε πρός σε θεῶν.—x. 289.

By all the Gods that rule the realms above,
By our young nuptials, by thy virgin love,
Be gentle, good, and kind. . . .
Nor leave me here, in jealous wrath, to lie
Sunk at thy feet, and miserably die
By such a cruel fate.

ŒNONE REPLIES.

'Αλλά μοι ἔρρε δόμοιο.—x. 324.

HENCE, traitor, from my home to Helen go;
There, night and day, worn out with ceaseless woe,
Lie murmuring on her bed, transfixed with grief,
Till her sweet soothing arts afford relief.

THE DEATH OF PARIS.

Πάριν δ' ἄρα θυμὸς ἐν Ἴδῃ.—x. 362.

So Paris died, nor Helen saw him more;
Him with wild shrieks the mountain Nymphs deplore,
Remembering in their gentle hearts the day
When he was foremost in their sportive play.
With them in heartfelt grief the herdsman mourned,
Till all the vales the shrill lament returned.

ŒNONE TOO LATE REPENTING OF HER CRUELTY.

Οἴη δ' ἐκ θυμοῖο δαίζατο.—x. 411.

NOR raised with Troy's sad dames the funeral strain,
But hid within her heart her lonely pain;
As on the lofty mountain's crest the snow
Dissolves in streams, and floods the plain below,
Touched by the Zephyr's melting breath, distil
The dropping cliffs in many a wandering rill;
And everywhere beneath the shady groves
Silent the cool, unfailing water roves.

* * * *οὐδέ τι θῆρας.*—x. 450.

Her, once so timid, now no more affright
The fierce and savage beasts that prowl by night;
She climbed each rugged mountain's dizzy brow,
Plunged fearless down the dark ravine below,
Where deep and black the dangerous torrents flow.
The moon looked down in pity from above,
Thought of her own Endymion's hapless love,
And, grieved to see her wildly, blindly stray,
Illumed with friendly light her weary way.

JUPITER INTERPOSING AMID THE CONFLICT OF THE GODS.

Διὸς δ' ἐπὶ πείρασι γαίης.—xii. 189.

YET 'scaped not these great Jove's all-seeing eye;
From ocean-bed he mounts the spacious sky.

Him all the winds, Eurus and Boreas bear,
Notus and Zephyrus, through the fields of air.
All these the many-coloured Iris brought,
And yoked them to the everlasting chariot, wrought
By old immortal Time's unwearied hand
Of living adamant. He took his stand
Upon Olympus' brow, and in his ire
Shook all the vault of heaven; 'mid lightning fire
On every side the volleying thunder peals,
While fast and thick to earth his bolts he deals.
Flames the wide air. The Gods in terror hear,
And shuddered each immortal limb with fear.

THE GRECIAN WARRIORS ISSUING FROM THE WOODEN HORSE.

καὶ ἐξ ἵπποιο χαμᾶζε.—xiii. 37.

Fain had each warrior leaped from out the steed,
He cautious still restrained their headlong speed.
Then gently, one by one, the bolts undid,
And opened slow the steed's close-fitted side.
And leaned a little forth, and peered around,
Lest any watchful Trojan kept the ground.
As from the hill the wolf, with hunger bold,
Descends, and prowls around the sleeping fold,
With his quick ear, stands, catching every sound,
Of watchful shepherd, or of startled hound;
And then, when all around is deathly mute,
Steals lightly o'er the fence with noiseless foot.

THE RETURN OF THE GREEKS.

THE CAPTIVES LOOK BACK FOR THE LAST TIME ON THEIR NATIVE SHORES.

ἀπὸ δὲ πρώρηθεν ἄνακτες.—xiv. 378.

Each chieftain from the prow
Poured the red wine upon the flood below,
Prayed for their safe return, but every prayer
Was lost, and mingled with the idle air.
But fondly still looked back the captive train,
On Ilion's shores, slow sinking in the main.
Unseen of their stern lords, that look they stole,
And gave to sorrow all the bleeding soul.
Some rested with their hands upon the knee,
Some smote their brows in wilder agony.
Th' unconscious babes nor mourned their captive fate
Nor their lost country's miserable state,
Their only care their mothers' flowing breast.
Ah youth, with ignorance of sorrow blest!
And all had wildly loosed their braidless hair,
And tore with frantic hands their bosoms bare.
Here on the cheek the frozen tear looked dry,
And here flowed frequent from the liquid eye.
They saw the flames that o'er the city broke,
And the dull volumes of all-wrapping smoke.
Still to Cassandra turned each wondering eye,
Thought on her oft-derided prophecy.
Smiling she sat amid the sorrowing crew,
Though deep within her heart was bursting too.

TRYPHIODORUS.

THE TAKING OF TROY.

ἐναιρομένων δ' ἄρα φώτων.—L. 8. Edit. Northmore.

AROUND, of many a slaughtered chieftain stand
The weary spear, the mute unthreatening brand;
Quenched is the breastplate's din, and ceased the sound
Of lance against the buckler's brazen round;
The bow unstrung, the arrows strew the ground.
The steed before the idle manger droops
Low his proud head and melancholy stoops;
Grieves for the partners of his fleet career,
Or mourns, with fond regret, the fallen charioteer.

Helen repeats the names of the warriors' wives and paramours as she moves in a sort of procession round the Trojan horse. The execution is better than the conception.

τὴν δὲ κιοῦσαν.—L. 465.

STATELY as she passed,
Troy's loose-robed dames their looks of wonder cast,
When Pallas' lofty fane she reached, amazed,
Before th' high-towering horse she stood and gazed.
Twice she walked round, and of some fair-haired dame,
Some Argive chieftain's wife, pronounced the name

With gentle voice. At every name beloved,
Almost to tears was some stern warrior moved,
Not all untouched, even Menelaus hears ;
Aigialeia's name melts Diomede to tears,
Penelope's made stern Ulysses groan.
But when Anticles heard that silvery tone,
That of his own Laodamia spoke,
Almost his answering lips the silence broke ;
But up Ulysses sprang, and hastily
Represt with both his hands th' unuttered cry.

COLUTHUS.

From the pretty Poem of Coluthus (Edit. Bekker)—the *Raptus Helenæ* —I give the distress of Helen's child, Hermione, when she misses her fugitive mother.

HERMIONE, her maiden veil withdrawn
And floating loose, beheld the opening dawn ;
And oft, the attendant damsels standing by,
She questions with a quick and eager cry :
" Where is she fled, and left me here to grieve ?
My mother ! where is she ? but yester-eve,
As was her wont, she took the chamber key,
And sweetly slumbered on one couch with me."
　　Weeping she spake, the maids stood weeping too ;
Before the gate, from every quarter, drew
The gentle Spartan dames, and vainly strove
To soothe the maiden with officious love.
" Weep not, sad child ! thy mother soon will come,
Ere yet thy tears are dry, unbidden, home.
Lo on thy cheeks the paleness grief has made !
Lo now thy youth's just opening roses fade !
At some gay bridal hath she passed the day,
And haply wandered on her homeward way ;
Or in the meads, 'midst flowers of sweetest hues,
Drinks the soft fragrance of the early dews ;
Or, having bathed in old Eurotas' tide,
Still lingers by the crystal water's side."

Weeping, she answered: "Kind, but most untrue!
Why speak ye thus? well every haunt she knew;
She knew each hill, each path she wont to tread,
And each byway that wound along the mead.
The dim stars sink, she sleeps on some wild hill;
The stars dawn bright, and she returns not still.
My mother! where is now thy lone retreat?
Where linger, on what cliff, thy tardy feet?
Ah! hast thou met the wild-beast's ravening jaw?
Yet beasts behold Jove's royal race with awe;
Or, headlong from thy stately car cast down,
Low in the dust, and mangled, art thou thrown?
But well the wood they tracked, thy form to see,
Searched every brake, and questioned every tree.
Unjustly we accuse the darksome wood!
Or hast thou sunk in blue Eurotas' flood?
The Naiads in each stream, in ocean deep,
Guiltless of woman's death, their vigils keep."

MUSÆUS.

HERO AND LEANDER.

THE FIRST MEETING.

Θαρσαλέως δ' ὑπ' Ἔρωτος.—L. 99. *Poetæ Græci Minores.*

Love made him bold; at once, all undismayed,
He glided in and stood before the maid,
And gazed on her with furtive eye askance,
Till her soul kindled at his voiceless glance.
She, as his rising passion she descried,
Stood up, rejoicing in her beauty's pride,
And now and then, almost concealed, a look
She stole towards the youth, that mutely spoke;
Then turned in haste away. Joy thrilled his breast
To see his love perceived and not repressed.

THE FIRST INTERVIEW.

Παρθενικὴ δ' ἄφθογγος.—L. 160.

Gazed on the earth the maid, and could not speak,
And strove to hide the blushes on her cheek;
And with her restless foot she beat the ground,
And closer drew her modest mantle round.
Sure omens all of love—for silence still,
Sweet rhetoric, speaks the maiden's yielding will.

At length, warm blushes purpling all her cheek,
To glad Leander she began to speak:—
  "Stranger, thy words might surely melt the stone;
Where hast thou learned that all-beguiling tone?
Alas, who led thee to my native land?

Yet idle all and vain thy words . . . .
In a tall tower my home, beside the sea,
With but one maid (my parents' harsh decree)
From Sestos' town afar, on the wild shore,
The only voice the ocean's booming roar.
Nor maiden friends approach my lone retreat,
Nor youthful choirs in jocund dances meet;
But, morn and night, the same deep sullen sound
Comes echoing from the wave-lashed rocks around."
  She said, and seeming her own speech to blame,
Hid in her robe her face, which burned with shame.

NONNUS.

Greek poetry—heathen Greek poetry—may be said to close with Nonnus. **Diffuse** to the most prodigal luxuriance, **feeble through his diffuseness**; the severe majesty, the graceful chastity, the effortless simplicity of Greek poetry has departed, and given place in Nonnus to an Asiatic copiousness and exuberance, to a heaping up of imagery, a redundant and effeminate versification, at which our English poetry seems rapidly arriving. Yet there is a richness of fancy, a splendour of diction, a harmony—if almost lascivious, yet singularly musical—which almost persuade us that in better times Nonnus might have been a great poet. One is curious to know how far he is indebted to the earlier poems on the mythic history of Bacchus. The Indian adventures almost remind us of the Indian poetry. Nonnus, it is well known (it is presumed that in his old age he became a Christian), wrote a poetical paraphrase on the Gospel of St. John. The flat feeble expansion and dilation of the exquisite simplicity of the Evangelist is far more wearisome, and is totally wanting in the lively fancifulness and fertility, the overflowing richness and harmony, of the Dionysiacs. We trust that Nonnus, as a **Christian, was a better** man, but fear that he was a much worse poet.

THE CONFLICT OF ARISTÆUS AND BACCHUS—
OF HONEY AND WINE.

ἀμφοτέροις δ' ἐδίκαζον.—xiii. 258. Edit. Falkenburg.

In solemn judgment sate
The dwellers in Olympus. Phœbus' son,
Offering the flowing liquor from the hive,
Lost the sweet victory. As their eager lips

The blossom-loving bees' thick nectar quaffed,
Palled on the taste the o'er-delicious dews;
With the third cup came full satiety;
The fourth stood all unpledged.   Then Bacchus drew
The foaming stream of all-inspiring wine,
And all the livelong day they sat and quaffed.

THE GARDEN IN SAMOTHRACE.

ὄρχατος ἔπλετο τοῖος —P. 57.

SUCH was that shady garden.   Near flowed forth
A fountain with two springs, whence all might draw
Perennial waters cool; in many a rill
Thence had the skilful gardener trained along
From plant to plant the winding wandering stream.
As through by Phœbus sent, the gentle fount
Went, softly murmuring round the laurel's root.
Each on his marble pedestal stood round
Many a tall youth, all subtly wrought in gold;
Each held a lamp, that threw its mellow light
O'er the evening banquet.   Rows of mimic dogs
Were scattered in the vestibule, and seemed
With open mouths, though mute, to bay; each hound
Of silver and of gold alternate stood,
As on their master fawning.   Each at once,
As Cadmus passed, appeared, with welcoming bay
Harmonious, to salute the godlike man,
And quiver with delight the unmoving tail.

THE PARTING OF HARMONIA FROM HER MOTHER AS BRIDE OF CADMUS.

καὶ κινυρῇ ῥαθάμιγγι.—P. 77.

HER cheeks all flowing with the frequent tear
Electra's face she kissed; her lips, her feet,
With lips less fond—her maiden modesty
Awed by her mother's presence. Then she pressed
Her sire Emathion's head, and breast, and cheek;
And folded all her maidens in her arms;
And even the senseless circle of the doors,
Her couch, and all her virgin chamber walls
Embraced; and, in her voiceless agony,
The very dust of her own native land.
Her by the hand (for so the Gods ordained)
Electra took, and gave the dowerless maid,
Harmonia, to her lord, and wiped away
Her mother's tears.

THE NURSING OF BACCHUS.

ἣ τότε Βάκχον ἑλοῦσα.—P. 165.

SHE from her breast divine young Bacchus took,
And unobserved in her dark caves concealed
The wondrous birth. Spontaneous, and at once,
The splendour of his radiant countenance
Proclaimed the Jove-born infant. All the walls
Of that dim palace whitened with the rays;

Shrank darkness from the intolerable light
That shone from Dionysus' brow. She sate
Night after night and watched the sleepless boy.
Oft feebly tottering on uncertain feet.
Young Melicerta to the other **breast**
Came nestling; her beside, the infant God
Lay murmuring "Evoë!" as he quaffed his food.
Then Mystes from her lady's breast received
And sleepless brooded o'er her godlike charge:
Mystes, whose name from mystic rites derived,
First Dionysus' midnight orgies taught;
And in Lyæus' wasteful rites the first
Shook the round tabor, and whirled high and **clashed**
The double brazen cymbal; kindling **first**
The flaming **pine-torch** o'er the midnight dance,
Shrieked "**Evoë! Evoë!**" round the unslumbering God.
First plucked the curling tendril of the vine
With the wild fillet round her braidless hair;
And with dark ivy wound her thyrsus wand;
Fearing the God to wound, its iron point
Sheathed careful with the mantling foliage. First
She **round her** naked bosom girt the wreath
Of brazen beads, the **fawn-skin round her loins**;
And taught the sportive boy the mysteries
Within the pregnant ark contained. She first
The zone of living vipers round her waist
Wound fearless; crept beneath **her breasts, and wreathed**
Its awful manacles the dragon coil.

BACCHUS AND AMPELUS.

Ἤδη γὰρ Φρυγίης ὑπὸ δειράδα.—P. 181.

For now beneath the Phrygian cliffs had grown
The blithe boy, Ampelus, Love's chosen flower.

Yet the soft down of the hyacinthine beard
Marked not the snowy round of his full cheek,
Youth's golden bloom.   Behind, his clustering hair
Over his ivory shoulders fell in curls
And braidless, lifted by the whispering breeze:

And through their knots profuse the neck of snow
Gleamed, faintly seen, as when the morn beams forth,
Half hidden, from behind some melting cloud.
His voice breathed honey through his rosy lips.
Spring was in all his form; where'er he moved
Beneath his silver feet the meadow bloomed
With roses; when his eloquent eyes glanced round
It was the radiant light of the full moon.

νέος δ' ἠγάλλετο θυμῷ.—P. 182.

   The youth rejoiced in soul,
Outshining thus his blooming peers. When sat
The boy beneath the shady mountain brake,
And wove his song, rapt Bacchus listening stood.
The boy away, he sat with smileless cheek.
If by the banquet board the Satyr danced,
And dancing beat his drum with jocund din,
That youth abroad to chase the bounding stag,
Loathed Bacchus the unwelcome merriment.
  * * * *

ἀλλ' ὅτε θύρσον ἄειρε.—P. 184.

But when the gallant boy would meet in fight
The raging bear, or on the lioness
Hurl his strong javelin, anxious, to the west
Looked the young God, lest Zephyr's fatal blast
Repel the shaft, as erst the envious Wind
Blew back with mortal force the heavy quoit
Against the gentle Hyacinthus' head.

THE BASSARIDES.

Βασσαρίδων δὲ φάλαγγες.—P. 264.

THEN first the wild Bassarides poured in
Their squadrons; as they gathered, one enwreathed
Her brows with snaky fillets, one her locks
With the wild ivy braided. There a maid
With brazen-pointed thyrsus armed her hand.
There stood, with unbound tresses floating loose,
The Mænalis, and all unveiled; the breeze
On both her shoulders lifted the long locks.
Another, as she shook her clustering hair,
Struck the loud tabor to the cymbal clang
Harmonious; one with many a frantic bound
Beat on the hollow leathern drum the din
Of mimic war: the thyrsi were their spears,
With the vine tendrils sheathed the brazen points.
Another for the bloody strife athirst,
Over her bosom clasped the brinded spoil
Of panther. Tunic-like her sister girt
The spotted hide of mountain-loving fawn,
Or robed her in the stag's dædalean skin.

THE RIVER CHANGED TO WINE.

ἀντιβίοις δ' ᾤκτειρε θεός.—P. 267.

COMPASSIONATE the gentle God beheld
The slaughter of his foes. In sportive mood

O'er all the stream he shed his joyous gift.
Swift their pale hue the yellow waters changed :
A nectar-breathing tide went murmuring down,
And all the flood ran wine.   The fragrant gales
Bore odours from the rich transmuted stream,
And smiled the empurpled shores.   The Indian bold
Drank, and broke forth in marvel : " Wondrous sight !
Strange but delicious draught ! surpassing far
The goat's white milk, or the dark fountain cool :
Nor such within his many-chambered cells
E'er works the humming bee : it flows along,
Joy to the soul, and fragrance to the sense !"

THE INDIANS DRINK THE STREAM.

δυσμενέας δ' ἐμέθυσσε.—P. 270.

From that delicious river all the foe,
Drunken and giddy with the frantic wine,
Rushed on the herd.   The Indian warrior seized,
'Mid the green brake, and led the menacing bull
Reluctant captive : both his daring hands
Grasped the twin horns.   Glorying, he dragged along
The horned Dionysus, so he deemed,
In triumph.   Here another held on high
His scythe-like falchion ; gashed, with rooked blade,
The throat of the wild mountain goat, and bore
Aloft, as 'twere, the severed head of Pan.
There one mowed down the heifer's lowing herd,

As 'twere the Satyr's slaughtered ranks. The next
Chased the fleet brood of branching-headed stags,
And gazing on their dappled skins, beheld
The wild Bassarides, in fawn-skins robed,
Lie panting underneath his conquering feet.

NICÆA.

ἔνθα τις ἀγκυλότοξος.—P. 275.

There, with bent bow, the child of desert glens,
The nursling of the forest, lived and bloomed,
Beauteous Nicæa, chaste as Artemis:
Like her, a maiden huntress, all averse
From love, in Cytheræa's arts untried.
O'er the wild hills she chased the savage game,
And track'd the bounding quarry. Not for her
The virgin chamber spread its incens'd roof.
Among the rugged rocks she made her couch.
Her distaff was the bow, her shafts she plied
For shuttles, and the web she wove, the snares
In which this mountain Pallas noosed her game,
The huntress Queen's companion undefiled.
No perfume reeked for her; the honied cup
Disdained she for the crystal fountain cool,
And o'er her unapproachèd palace arched
The mountain cave. Oft weary with the chase,
She couched beneath the panther, or at morn
Under the shadowy rock reposed her head

Close by the nursing lioness: the beast
With tranquil eye half-closed, reclined, and licked,
With fangs unharming, her smooth skin ; or like
Some faithful watch-dog, with low bay supprest,
Lay murmuring, deeming 'twas **Diana's self.**
Drooping to earth the terror of his mane
And shaggy neck, the lion couched and slept.

NICÆA OVERPOWERED WITH WINE.

καὶ φρένα δινηθεῖσα.—P. 296.

ALL giddy with the draught, the maid 'gan rave,
And to and fro she shook her whirling head,
And with her wandering eyes she thought she saw
Two lakes their crystal surface spread below,
And every crag, as heavy sank her head,
Doubled and multiplied around. At length,
Soft sliding with her trembling foot, she fell
Under the wing of sleep; her failing knees
Sank: o'er the virgin spread the bridal trance.

THE CAPTURE OF THE WARRIOR DERIADES.

καὶ θεὸς ἀφραίνοντα.— P. 598.

THE frantic chief, thus warring 'gainst the gods,
Himself divine, young Ampelus beheld.
Sudden a strange ally, a vine, sprang up:
Gently around the silver-wheeled car

Curled up the growing tendrils; till at length
Around Deriades himself were wound
The green indissoluble **chains.** It spread,
Clustering its dark grapes o'er the lofty brow
Of the idly-raging **king. The rich festoons**
Hung **o'er** his helmet, and their fragrance **breathed**
A sweet intoxication as they coiled;
And with no iron fetters bound him down
Motionless, hand and foot and limb. In vain
Struggled the unwieldy elephants, their feet
Were rooted with unyielding ivy-bands,
That bound them **to the earth; not half so firm**
The remora, that sheathes **its crooked** fang
In the ship's side, detains th' unmoving bark.
Shouted in vain the charioteer, and lashed
Their disobedient backs with the fierce **goad**
Of his sharp scourge. Thus whom the warrior lance
Subdued not, India's mighty king, **the Vine,**
A sterner foe, took captive.

THE TRIUMPH.

καὶ χορὸς ἄσπετος ἔσκεν.—P. 678.

COUNTLESS the choral dance, the Bassaris
First trod the maddening plain with sandal'd foot.
With heavy heel and sidelong movement rude
The Satyr bounded; on the snowy neck
Of some wild Bacchanal wound his coarse arm,
And whirled her round and round. The doubling drum
Beat, and the warrior chieftains, all in arms,
In many a mazy circle spinning round,
Mimicked the shielded Corybantic dance.
The helmed choir the horsemen joined, and hymned
All-conquering Bacchus. Noiseless was there none;
Soared to the seven-zoned heaven the Evian song.

* * καὶ δηίων ὅλον ὄλβον.—P. 679.

And all the plundered wealth of that rich land
The warriors bore—the Indian jasper, ores,

Pencilled and dark like hyacinthine flowers,
And pale smaragdus. Some from 'neath the cliffs
Of steep Imaus drove the stately hosts
Of captive elephants ; while others rode
Aloft in Indian chariots, lion-drawn.
These to the yoke the brindled panther bowed,
And home went hastening to Mygdonia's streams
Triumphant. Here the revelling Satyr sped,
And with his scourge of vine-twigs lashed along
The spotted tiger. One the fragrant plant
Which fishers cull, bore to his favourite Nymph
In Cybele's wild train, or that bright gem,
The wonder of the Erythrean sea.
And many a sable bride was dragged along
With her scarce-wedded bridegroom, torn away
Even from her nuptial chamber. So they passed
To Tmolus' heights, the Bacchanalian rout,
Hymning great Evan as he home returned.
And multitudes were there that bore the gems
With which the Indian seas are all inlaid,
And birds of myriad hue.

BACCHUS LOOKING UPON TYRE.

καὶ πτόλιν ἀθρήσας.— P. 681.

JOYFUL he gazed on that fair city. Her
Had Neptune girded with a zone of waves
Not wholly. Such her heavenly form as shows

The moon to fulness verging, yet not full.
He looked upon the mingling sea and land
With new amaze. For 'mid the sea Tyre lies,
Yet not from earth dissevered. The waves wash
Three sides; a narrow belt links her to land.
Firm fixed she lay, as some fair Nymph that swims,
Her head, her neck, her breast, her hands outspread
Upon the level waters; on each side
Glitters and sparkles the white foam; yet still
Cling to her mother earth her rooted feet;
Still Neptune binds her in his liquid chains,
Or, a glad bridegroom, swims around, and clasps
With murmuring arms the maiden's snowy neck.
   The God was lost in wonder. Here alone
The herdsman, piping on the beach, breaks off
His song, and with the neighbouring sailor holds
Close converse; and the goatherd may salute
The fisher as he hauls his net. The plough
Cleaves the hard earth; a little way below
The answering oar is furrowing the broad sea.
   Long time he gazed, and then in wondering speech
Broke forth: "Is this an isle, or continent
I gaze on? here the Hamadryad hears
The Nereid singing o'er the moonlit sea.
Over the Tyrian bay, and cultured shores
Breaking from Lebanus, the noonday gale
Freshens the bending grain, and wafts the barks.
Cooling the husbandman's and sailor's brow.

MYTHOLOGICAL HYMN.

ἀστροχίτων Ἡρακλες.—P. 683.

O STAR-ROBED Hercules! the Lord of fire!
The ruler of the world! the Pastor thou
Of shadowy mortal life! or if that name,
The Sun, delight thee! Through th' empyreal heaven
With burning orb career'st thou, and unfold'st
The Son of Time, the twelve moon'd year, revolved
Round after round; and from thy chariot flow
Cycles for aye renewed from youth to age.
In subtle travail, with no mother's aid,
Thou bringest forth an image of thyself,
A rounded orb: what time the dewy moon
Milks from thy pregnant rays reflected light,
Till her horned crescent gathers its full blaze.
  All glorious eye of heaven! thy four-wheeled car,
After the glowing autumn, winter leads;
To summer warms the spring. Unstable Night
Before thy arrowy torch retreats apace;
While, yet half-seen, thy proud steeds' lofty neck,
Drawing the snowy yoke, is onward lashed.
And as thou blazest brighter, heaven's rich mead
No more is charactered with glittering stars.
Thou plungest in the deep Atlantic. Soon
Shaking thy fertilizing locks, undried,

The teeming shower distill'st thou. Earth breathes up
The airy moisture of her early dews.
    Belus by old Euphrates! Ammon named
In sable Libya! Apis by the Nile!
Kronus the Arabians' God! **Assyrian Jove!**
To thy rich-odoured shrine the fragrant wood
That wise and ancient bird of ages brings,
The Phœnix, that in death begets herself
(True everlasting emblem **she of time**)
To a new life, and in the funeral pyre
Casts off the slough of **age,** and in that pyre
Renews her youth.
                  And wert thou **not again**
The Egyptians' **cloudless** Jove, Serapis? Thou
Art **Saturn! many-namèd** Phaethon!
Mithra, and **Babylonian El ; in Greece,
Delphic Apollo. Love art thou,**
All-healing Pæan, **and the dædal sky
Art thou!** most fitly named **star-robed! for still
The midnight sky assumes her starry vest.
Propitious hear, great God! my solemn vow.**

AGAVE WITH THE HEAD OF PENTHEUS.

ἡ δὲ μεταστρέψασα νόον.—P. 787.

      RECOVERED slow
Her wandering mind and long incredulous sight ;
There, rooted to the earth and voiceless, stood
The mother. That wan head she saw, she knew—
'Twas Pentheus'. Down she fell ; her snowy locks
Defiling in the dust, she lay and rolled ;
The shaggy garment of the God rent off
From her indignant bosom, the bead-zone
Of that wild Thyasus ; and all her breast,
Her inmost bosom's unseen folds ran blood.
Her son's closed eye she kissed, his cheeks' pale round,
The rich hair on his bloody brow, and shrieked
In this wild strain : " Relentless God, and most
To thine own race relentless ! give me back
My madness, for I now am worse than mad.
Give me my phrenzy. Let me call him still
The savage beast, and not my murdered son."

Printed by R. CLARK, Edinburgh.

www.ingramcontent.com/pod-product-compliance
Lightning Source LLC
Chambersburg PA
CBHW030002240426
43672CB00007B/793